Lucy

AND HER TIMES

Pascal Picq
Nicole Verrecchia

A Henry Holt Reference Book
Henry Holt and Company
New York

A
PICTURE
IS WORTH
A THOUSAND
WORDS

Xun Zi (313-238 B.C.)

A Henry Holt Reference Book
Henry Holt and Company, Inc.
Publishers since 1866
115 West 18th Street
New York, New York 10011

Henry Holt® is a registered trademark
of Henry Holt and Company, Inc.

Library of Congress Cataloging-in-Publication Data
Picq, Pascal G.
[Lucy et son temps. English]
Lucy and her times/Pascal Picq and Nicole Verrechia.—1st
American ed.
p. cm.
—(A Henry Holt Reference book)
(W5 (who, what, where, when, and why))
Includes bibliographical references and index.
1. Australopithecus afarensis—Pictorial works. 2. Fossil
man—Africa—Pictorial works. 3. Fossil man—Ethiopia—
Pictorial works. 4. Man—Origin—Pictorial works.
I. Verrechia, Nicole. II. Title. III. Series.
IV. Series: W5 (who, what, where, when, and why) series.
GN283.25.P5313 1996   96-28393
569'.9—dc20   CIP

ISBN 0-8050-5062-0

Henry Holt books are available for special
promotions and premiums.
For details contact: Director, Special Markets.

Originally published in France in 1996 by
Editions Mango under the title *Lucy et son temps*.
First published in the United States in 1996
by Henry Holt and Company, Inc.

First American Edition—1996

Idea and series by Dominique Gaussen
American English translation by Constantin Marinescu
Consultant: Donald C. Johanson, Ph.D.
Typesetting by Jay Hyams and Christopher Hyams Hart

Printed in Italy by G. Canale & C. S.p.A. - Borgaro T.se - TURIN
All first editions are printed on acid-free paper. ∞

1 2 3 4 5 6 7 8 9 10

30 MYA
*Expansion
of modern primates*

20 MYA
The golden age of hominoids

37 MYA
*The great break and extinction
of archaic mammals*

50 MYA
*Expansion
of mammals*

60 MYA
CENOZOIC ERA
Age of mammals

THE SPIRAL OF TIME

70 MYA
*Extinction of dinosaurs
and development of
flowering plants*

100 MYA
*Diversification
of primitive mammals*

150 MYA
*First birds
take flight*

170 MYA
*Expansion
of dinosaurs*

200 MYA
*Reptilian
mammals*

220 MYA
MESOZOIC ERA –
Expansion of reptiles

250 MYA
*Expansion
of amphibians*

300 MYA
*Vast carboniferous
forests*

350 MYA
*Vertebrates
move onto land*

400 MYA
*Plants and insects
move onto land*

455 MYA
*Vascular
plants*

550 MYA
*First
vertebrates*

570 MYA
PALEOZOIC ERA

600 MYA**
*Sponges, jellyfish,
and algae*

3 MYA
Lucy

200,000 YEARS AGO
Modern humans

12 BYA*
BIG BANG
Birth of the universe

4.5 BYA
Formation
of the solar system
and Earth

3 BYA
Bacteria and
primitive algae

2 BYA
Single-celled
organisms

1 BYA
Nucleated
cells

WHAT WAS IT LIKE BEFORE THERE WAS A BEFORE?

This simple diagram represents the parade of life on Earth, a parade about 3 billion years long. Life makes its debut on Earth shortly after the formation of the planet around 4.5 billion years ago. The first life forms are molecules capable of duplicating themselves; these are followed by bacteria and then—around 1 billion years ago—cells with a nucleus.

THE OCEAN BECOMES THE FIRST "IN" PLACE

Life begins developing around 3 billion years ago, and it begins in the sea: the most primitive organisms move in water. The process gets in gear with single-celled organisms, bacteria and primitive algae, but by about 1 billion years ago these have joined to form multicellular organisms, such as algae, sponges, and jellyfish. By then, the world's oceans are teeming with these creatures. The ocean is the "in" place to be—the only place—a special environment where the first creatures equipped with organs appear around 700 million years ago. Around 500 million years ago a special group of creatures evolves, animals whose bodies are organized around an axis: the spinal column. Never have the seas seen such things, these amazing vertebrates! With time, however, there is a traffic jam: the aquatic stage becomes too crowded for all these actors. But among all these creatures are some highly innovative ones with lungs enabling them to breath in the air as well as in water and endowed with stiffened, muscular fins, early versions of legs. These find they can leave the water to check out the action on dry land. Indeed, at the end of the Paleozoic Era, they gather their courage and take this momentous step. It is this step that heralds the age of amphibians, which then romp through the huge carboniferous forests (by then plants and insects have already made their way out of the water and created a landscape).

JURASSIC PARK MOVES IN

Content with life on dry land, some of these bold creatures abandon their amphibious ways and evolve into reptiles. A few million years later, we come upon the Mesozoic Era, where the billboard for Jurassic Park proudly announces its new star performers: the dinosaurs. Mammals, which until then have been only extras in this play of life, flourish with the coming of flowering plants. These plants and fruit-bearing trees provide an ideal environment for these early mammals, around 55 million years ago. The primates begin spreading around 30 million years ago, and the family of the hominids, our family, announces itself sometime around 15 million years ago. Lucy and her species begin to appear on the horizon around 4 million years ago. The history of modern humans plays only a small role in this grand drama of life, not even 1 million years, and all of that just might be due to Lucy. Stay tuned; we'll find out.

* BYA : **BILLION YEARS AGO**
** MYA : **MILLION YEARS AGO**

THIS IMAGE IS FLATTERING BUT FALSE

Humans are so wonderful that all of nature exists for them alone. All of the long history of evolution, from the dawn of time onward, had only one ultimate goal: HUMAN BEINGS.

This notion, based on an idea called the process of "hominization" (see illustration below), is an erroneous idea that abandons various groups of apes along the long march of evolution. According to this old formulation only humans reach the highest stage of evolution, in which their brainy (and also thick) skull is held high atop a body standing proudly erect. Hominization caters to the pride of what is obviously the most intelligent species, but not necessarily the most evolved. By eliminating the false concepts of hominization, one discovers the different and fascinating family history in the picture opposite.

THIS IMAGE IS LESS FLATTERING BUT TRUE

Without doubt, humans have plenty of reasons to look on themselves as particularly well-endowed apes. But monkeys and apes—if one could enter their minds—probably wouldn't think less about themselves. All of today's monkeys are the result of evolution. From the point of view of mother nature, there is no reason to consider any one species more or less primitive than others. Consequently none of them, even those closest to us, looks anything like Lucy or one of our other ancestors. After all, one can be the offspring only of parents, not of a brother or cousin.

Fossils, like Lucy, contain general characteristics that are found in all "family" members (whether chimpanzees, humans, or gorillas), but they also have their own very specific characteristics. And that's the charm of our ancestors!

SO WHO'S THE MONKEY'S UNCLE?

Classifying species might seem like child's play. Just put all those that seem the most alike in one group, create another group for all those that exhibit other distinct similarities, and so on. The game can quickly become quite complicated, however, if you decide to change the characteristics you're using to form different groups or if you are out to prove the validity of a theory. The problem is that researchers rarely start with the same ideas, and the subject of gene theory often gets in the way. These versions of the human family tree show what can go wrong or right.

TRADITIONAL OR GRADUALIST TREE PRUNED FOR HOMINIZATION

Gibbon   Orangutan   Gorilla   Chimpanzee   Human

In this tree the chimpanzee and gorilla are brothers, with the orangutan as a cousin. In turn, all these big apes are first cousins to humans. The gibbon is placed on a separate branch as a distant cousin. This family tree seems tidy but is completely incorrect.

TREE BASED ON CERTAIN GENES AND BEHAVIORAL PATTERNS

Gibbon   Orangutan   Gorilla   Chimpanzee   Human

In this version humans and chimpanzees are brothers; the gorilla is their cousin. All of them have the orangutan as first cousin. The gibbon is again on the most remote branch. This tree brings to light the very strong resemblances between humans and chimpanzees at the genetic and behavioral levels.

TRULY WARPED FAMILY TREE BASED ON A CONFUSION OF DATA

Gibbon   Orangutan   Gorilla   Chimpanzee   Human

When you try to please everybody, you'll never recognize your brothers! The gorilla, chimpanzee, and human are all brothers here. The orangutan is their first cousin. As for the gibbon, he's out on his usual separate branch.

TREE BASED ON DIFFERENT GENES AND ANATOMY

Gibbon   Orangutan   Gorilla   Chimpanzee   Human

This is the tree we prefer. The chimpanzee and gorilla are brothers; humans are their cousin. All the species from Africa are first cousins of the orangutan, which is from Asia. The gibbon is again relegated to the most remote branch.

8

THIS IMAGE

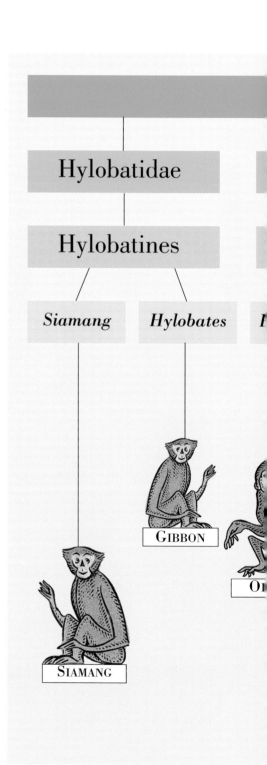

Hylobatidae

Hylobatines

Siamang   Hylobates

GIBBON

SIAMANG

DESERVES A BIT OF ATTENTION

(You are a *Homo sapiens*, aren't you?)

In order to find our way among these family relationships we must climb the tree. The superfamily of the Hominoidea comprises the humans and modern apes (and their extinct ancestors). It is made up of the families of the hylobatids, pongids, and hominids; each family includes subfamilies; and beneath the subfamilies are the genera. The next smallest unit is the species.

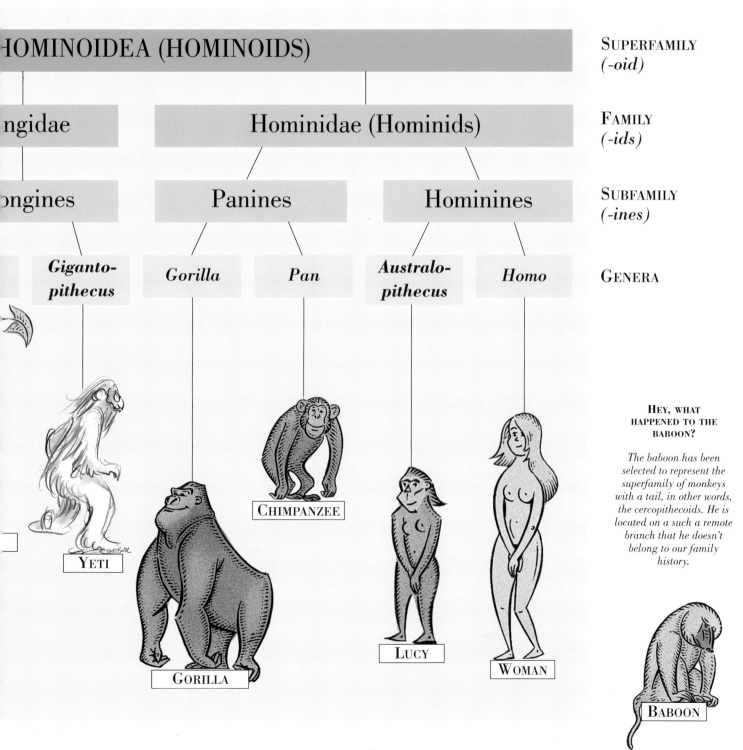

HOMINOIDEA (HOMINOIDS)		SUPERFAMILY (*-oid*)
ngidae	Hominidae (Hominids)	FAMILY (*-ids*)
ongines	Panines	Hominines	SUBFAMILY (*-ines*)
Giganto-pithecus	*Gorilla*	*Pan*	*Australo-pithecus*	*Homo*	GENERA

YETI

GORILLA

CHIMPANZEE

LUCY

WOMAN

HEY, WHAT HAPPENED TO THE BABOON?

The baboon has been selected to represent the superfamily of monkeys with a tail, in other words, the cercopithecoids. He is located on a such a remote branch that he doesn't belong to our family history.

BABOON

名詞は何の役に立つのでしょうか。物を明確

ます。しかし、存在する多くの言語の中には

するために異なる名詞があります。同じ物の

なります。それで各々の種にラテン語の名を

同一の名詞を共有することが可能となり

あるゆえ、名詞が変化するおそれがありませ

に、*Macaca fuscata* のラテン語が見られるの

ついて語ろうとしている訳です。

What's a name for? Why, to name, of course! But since each of the thousands of languages in our world uses a different name to designate things like cats, dogs, and flowers, there are thousands of names for each thing around us. In order to organize the vast number of plants and animals into categories that can be named and discussed, a Latin name has been given to each species. Thus in the middle of a Japanese text the Latin name *Macaca fuscata* stands out because its author is discussing the macaques from Japan.

This way of naming species using two Latin words is called binomial nomenclature. The system combines the name of a genus (a group of related species) with that of a species, and it is used for the world of plants and animals.

For example, the domestic dog and the wolf both belong to the genus *Canis*; the dog is *Canis familiaris*, the wolf is *Canis lupus*. Lucy's official name is *Australopithecus afarensis*; the genus name means "southern ape," and her species name, *afarensis*, is a Latinized form of Afar, the region in Ethiopia where she was found. Using only the name of the species, *afarensis*, would be vague since there are *Australopithecus afarensis* (Lucy), *Kolpochoerus afarensis* (a kind of wart hog, also from Afar), the *Hipparion afarense* (a cousin of the horse), and even others. To avoid confusion, the genus name (*Australopithecus*, *Hipparion*) must be used together with that of the species. The name of the genus always begins with a capital letter, that of

THAN CAT AND DOG

見分けるのためのものであり

ぞれ人間、犬、花等を名指し

記すため、言葉が膨大な数に

ることにより、全ての人々が

す。またラテン語は死語で

従って日本語のテキストの中

著者が日本のマカツク猿に

THE AUTHOR STATES HIS TITLES

"I'm a member in good standing of the species Homo sapiens. *As a point of honor, I never give my titles without reference to my noble genus, the genus* Homo. *I never answer when called by anything less, certainly not when called by only my species name. So don't try to get friendly with me by calling me just* sapiens, *I won't say boo to you, and anyway you'd be wrong in more senses than just the scientific. I'm also a member in good standing of a more intimate group, the subspecies* Homo sapiens sapiens. *If there's time I could also cite my other titles: subfamily of the hominines, family of the hominids (Hominidae), superfamily (and it is) of the hominoids (Hominoidea) infraclass of the catarrhines (Catarrhini), subclass of the anthropoids (Anthropoids), order of primates (Primates), class of mammals (Mammalia) in the animal kingdom (of which I consider myself king), phylum of the Chordata, and, finally, inhabitant of the planet Earth, fifth largest planet of the solar system, third in order from the Sun . . . "*

My name is Australopithecus afarensis, but you can call me Lucy!

the species with a lowercase letter. The name of a subspecies follows the species. The genus name may be abbreviated after its first mention—after citing *Homo sapiens*, you can refer to *H. sapiens*. This is the only authorized official "jargon."

This method of naming and classifying species, used today by naturalists and biologists throughout the world, is based on the work the great Swedish naturalist Carolus Linnaeus (yes, indeed, his name is Latin; he was born Karl Linné, but once he got started Latinizing things he got a little carried away). Linnaeus placed humans in the order of the primates in 1758 and gave us our name: *Homo sapiens*.

ORANGUTAN, *alias* **Pongo pygmaeus**
"Like you modern humans, I'm the sole living representative of a family that was once quite large and that flourished in Asia more than 15 million years ago. My name comes from a Malay word meaning 'forest person,' and it wasn't so long ago that you humans thought we were your closest kin. Now you prefer the African apes, or at least that's what I hear."

ZINJ, *alias* **Australopithecus boisei**
"In this family snapshot I represent the tribe of the hyperrobust australopithecines. We were numerous in East Africa between 2.5 and 1 million years ago. Our powerful jaws give us the nickname 'nutcracker man.' The other hominids were not really better developed. We lived together for a long time, but eventually we died out."

THE MAN WITH NICE JAWS, *alias* **Homo rudolfensis**
"We men from the period preceding 2 million years ago started out by chewing hard. Modern men with their delicate jaws and their ridiculously authoritarian chins had difficulties in recognizing me."

THE NEWCOMER, *alias* **Homo ergaster**
"I'm more or less like H. habilis, more or less like H. erectus; my species name means 'work man,' because I may have used stone tools. I've always been proud, always stood up tall—the better to see where I was."

THE STANDING MAN, *alias* **Homo erectus**
"Modern humans should be grateful to me— you guys owe me everything: fire, the conquest of the ancient world, efficient tools. In short, I'm humanity in progress."

CHIMPANZEE, *alias* **Pan troglodytes**
"I share 98 percent of my genes with the bonobo chimpanzee and humans: pretty impressive, eh? What all that means is that we have a common ancestor, and that ancestor . . . well, it wasn't me."

TWIGGY, *alias* **Homo habilis**
"I'm a master of stone work—my species name means 'handy man'—even if I use stones only to crack nuts. And I'm very happy to point out that my braincase was the largest of any hominid my age or older."

GORILLA, *alias* **Gorilla gorilla**
"There was a time when humans believed their ancestors had been large apes like me or my pal, the chimpanzee. That's because we still live in Africa, where ancient humans are thought to have come into existence. Even so, they were wrong."

LUCY, *alias* **Australopithecus afarensis**
"Here I am, the star of this book. I wasn't alone around 3 million years ago: there were also the Australopithecus anamensis, my cousins from Chad, and those from South Africa. And what would you say if I told you that I did not stay in Afar, in Ethiopia, but I traveled a lot on my little legs, and that . . ."

PORTRAIT
FIVE MILLION YEARS IN A SINGLE PHOTO!

PYGMY CHIMPANZEE OR BONOBO, *alias* **Pan paniscus**
"Humans call me pygmy. Ridiculous! I'm not that much smaller than my buddy the 'regular' chimpanzee. As for my sexual and social habits, well, they're said to be reminiscent of human behavior. So I ask you: who came first? Who's 'aping' whom?"

GIBBON, *alias* **Hylobates lar**
"Just thought I'd drop by. Get it? I come a long way, from the beautiful tropical forests of southern Asia where I live these days. We gibbons belong to the most remote branch of this huge superfamily. But we're hanging on!"

THE AUSTRALOPITHECINE WOMAN OF THE ROOTS, *alias* **Ardipithecus ramidus**
"On account of my advanced age—4.4 million years—it's hardly surprising that I share characteristics with both the chimpanzee and Lucy. I, too, lived in the trees at a time when Afar in Ethiopia was a much greener place."

NEANDERTAL MAN, *alias* **Homo sapiens neanderthalensis**
"Here I am, and delighted to be here, though I am a little surprised. Ever since scientists discovered me, they've cast me in many roles, and they still do. These days they say I'm a great European who lived and evolved on that continent for hundreds of thousands of years before mysteriously vanishing away 30,000 years ago. But here I am!"

MODERN WOMAN, *alias* **Homo sapiens sapiens**
"I suppose we humans exaggerate when we call ourselves 'smart smart'—that's what sapiens sapiens means, you know. Scientists have gone to a lot of trouble to give everyone in this family a special name, but I think Lucy's is the best. She's very nice, but she sure is a chatterbox . . ."

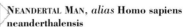

THE AUSTRALOPITHECINE WOMAN FROM LAKE TURKANA, *alias* **Australopithecus anamensis**
"What a name! All it means is that I was found near the shores of Lake Turkana in Kenya. Life was great in that pleasant corner of the world 4.1 million years ago. I've been known only since the summer of 1995. They say I've got the head of an ancestor of Lucy and the legs of a modern human; my mother always said I had her eyes. Frankly speaking, I have my doubts about the spot they've found for me in this big old family. But you know the way scientists are."

MRS. PLES, *alias* **Australopithecus africanus**
"I'm the one from South Africa, and Lucy is the one from East Africa—but we didn't live in isolation. Between 3 and 2.5 million years ago members of my clan, A. africanus, and members of hers, A. afarensis, were spread around just about everywhere, not to mention our new pal from Chad, the intriguing Abel."

ABEL, *alias* **Australopithecus bahrelghazalia**
"There's something new west of the African Rift, and that's me. I was discovered only in 1995, but I've already made a mess of the theories of paleoanthropologists. They found nothing more than my lower jaw, but that was enough—some of my teeth are like those of humans, and some are like those of apes. Pay no attention to that fancy Latin name— they made it up from the name of a riverbed near where I was waiting to be found. Just call me Abel."

BABOON, *alias* **Papio papio**
"Thank goodness! Really, I'm out of my wits with joy at not being included in that unruly bunch. Can you believe that some humans think apes are a primitive group? What's the big deal about standing upright all the time? Isn't that always the way in big families!"

OUT OF AFRICA; OR, ALL BABIES COME FROM THE SAME CRADLE

Remains of the earliest direct ancestors of human beings have been found in one place only: Africa. Today, most scientists believe that early ancestors of modern humans came into being in Africa and spread from there throughout the rest of the world. This theory is further supported by the fact that the big apes that are most closely related to modern humans are the gorillas and chimpanzees of Africa, indicating that human origins must also be placed on that continent. But how closely are humans related to those big apes? Researchers carried out an investigation using genes. Genes are the tiny elements that are at least partially responsible for what you are. Brothers and sisters in the same family have many more genes in common with each other than they have in common with their first cousins, and those first cousins have more in common with each other than with second cousins. The same kind of sharing can be found in larger groups, such as species; in fact, the study of genes can help determine the members of a given species. The more genes certain species have in common, the closer their kinship relation and the more likely they are to have a common ancestor. The common ancestor of two sister species is more recent than the ancestor of two cousin species, and so on. Based on all this, one can say that the big African apes are our "cousins" and that the orangutans are our "cousins." Chimps, bonobo chimps, gorillas, and humans have in common 98 percent of their genes. From that fact it's clear that our common ancestor lived not so long ago—sometime between 5 and 10 million years ago.

THE OLDEST FOSSILS ARE IN AFRICA

Lucy is "only" 3.2 million years old, but fossils belonging to her species have been found in East Africa covering the time span between 4 and 3 million years ago. Nearly as old are fossils of *Australopithecus africanus* from South Africa and remains of another species, known as Abel, in Chad, west of the African Rift. Another australopithecine, *A. anamensis*, was living in modern Kenya around 4 million years ago. *Ardipithecus ramidus* from Ethiopia is dated to around 4.4 million years ago. Fossils have been found in East Africa that date to between 6 and 5 million years ago; unfortunately, they are too fragmentary for scientists to give them a name, but they're hominid, of that there's no doubt. Let's cut to the chase: remains of hominids dating to between 4 and 3 million years ago have been found all over Africa; even more ancient fossils, dating to between 5 and 4 million years ago, have been found in East Africa, along with a few that date to between 6 and 5 million years ago.

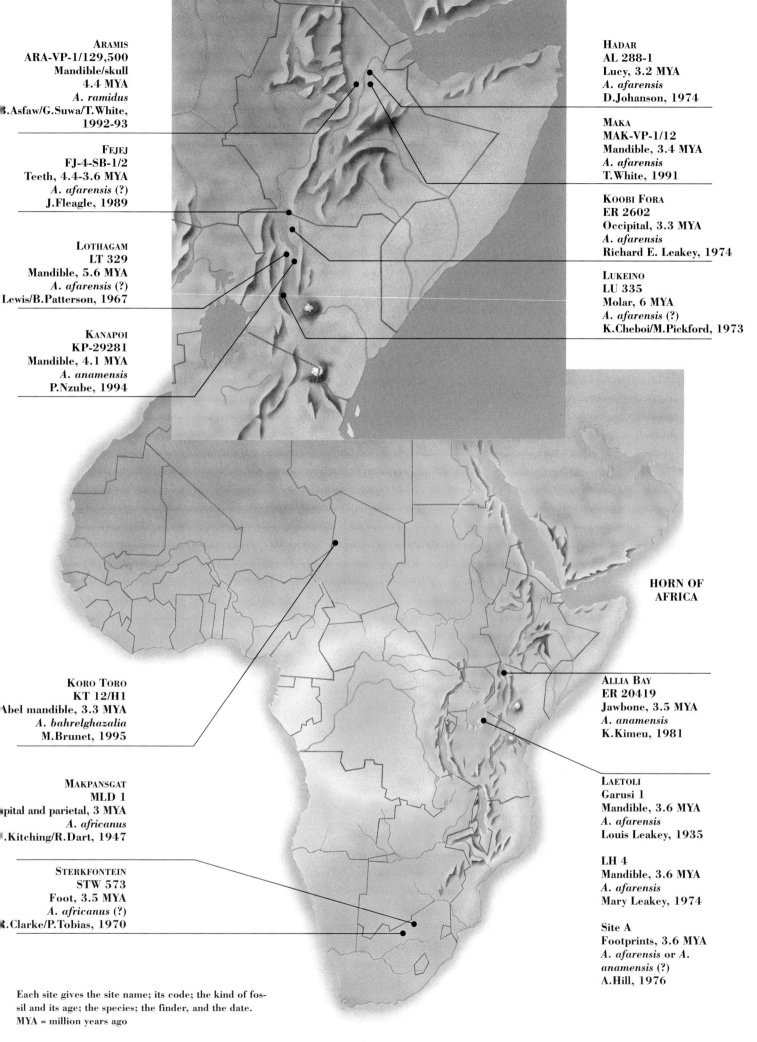

ARAMIS
ARA-VP-1/129,500
Mandible/skull
4.4 MYA
A. ramidus
B.Asfaw/G.Suwa/T.White,
1992-93

FEJEJ
FJ-4-SB-1/2
Teeth, 4.4-3.6 MYA
A. afarensis (?)
J.Fleagle, 1989

LOTHAGAM
LT 329
Mandible, 5.6 MYA
A. afarensis (?)
Lewis/B.Patterson, 1967

KANAPOI
KP-29281
Mandible, 4.1 MYA
A. anamensis
P.Nzube, 1994

HADAR
AL 288-1
Lucy, 3.2 MYA
A. afarensis
D.Johanson, 1974

MAKA
MAK-VP-1/12
Mandible, 3.4 MYA
A. afarensis
T.White, 1991

KOOBI FORA
ER 2602
Occipital, 3.3 MYA
A. afarensis
Richard E. Leakey, 1974

LUKEINO
LU 335
Molar, 6 MYA
A. afarensis (?)
K.Cheboi/M.Pickford, 1973

**HORN OF
AFRICA**

KORO TORO
KT 12/H1
Abel mandible, 3.3 MYA
A. bahrelghazalia
M.Brunet, 1995

MAKPANSGAT
MLD 1
Occipital and parietal, 3 MYA
A. africanus
J.Kitching/R.Dart, 1947

STERKFONTEIN
STW 573
Foot, 3.5 MYA
A. africanus (?)
R.Clarke/P.Tobias, 1970

ALLIA BAY
ER 20419
Jawbone, 3.5 MYA
A. anamensis
K.Kimeu, 1981

LAETOLI
Garusi 1
Mandible, 3.6 MYA
A. afarensis
Louis Leakey, 1935

LH 4
Mandible, 3.6 MYA
A. afarensis
Mary Leakey, 1974

Site A
Footprints, 3.6 MYA
A. afarensis or *A.
anamensis* (?)
A.Hill, 1976

Each site gives the site name; its code; the kind of fossil and its age; the species; the finder, and the date.
MYA = million years ago

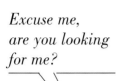

Excuse me, are you looking for me?

HERE, FOSSIL,

Early in the twentieth century, scientists construct an image of what comes to be known as the missing link, meaning fossil evidence of a being half-man and half-ape. Such a fossil would prove the "link" between apes and man; scientists think it would have the body of an ape and the large brain characteristic of humans. They believe the development of humans—the process of hominization—must have started with a large brain and that the body just followed suit. The much-awaited fossil is "found" in 1912 by William Dawson in a gravel pit at Piltdown in Sussex, England: pieces of a humanlike skull with an apelike jaw that become famous as Piltdown man. The scientific community, along with a large public audience, is fascinated by this relic, which seems to provide positive proof of evolutionary theory. It seems too good to be true—and it is, although the truth isn't revealed until 1954. As it turns out, this is merely

FOSSIL, HERE, FOSSIL, FOSSIL . . .

a hoax, some unknown person took a human skull and an orangutan's jaw, broke them up and stained them brown to make them look old, and then buried them near where Dawson was digging.

Another "missing link" shows up in 1924, this time in a far corner of South Africa, where the anatomist Raymond Dart finds a child's skull—today known as the Taung child, after the area where it was found—that has both hominid and ape characteristics. Dart gives the skull the name *Australopithecus*, meaning "southern ape," because he believes it was a kind of ape. Subsequent discoveries prove otherwise: Dart had found and named a genus of early hominids. This becomes evident after discoveries of other australopithecine species at Sterkfontein (1936), Makpansgat (1947), Kromdrai (1938), and Swartkrans (1947). These discoveries support Dart's theory, based on ideas from Charles Darwin, that human evolution began in Africa. This theory also proposes a different order of evolution, one in which our human ancestors first assumed the bipedal position—walked upright—and that the large brain developed later. Despite all the fossils discovered between 1924 and 1959, the importance of *Australopithecus* is not recognized; in fact, many scientists cling to the theory that Asia was the "cradle of mankind." The moral of the story: just as one swallow doesn't make spring, a single fossil, even a small pile, can't change ideas of evolution—at least not right away.

They look for me, and they find me, time and again!

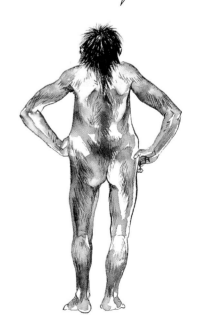

THE MISSING LINK

(IT'S STILL MISSING!)

The missing link, that piece in the chain of evolution joining humans to apes, has long fascinated both scientists and the public at large: are humans really related to apes? Can humans possibly be half-human and half-animal? The famous psychiatrist Sigmund Freud believed that neurosis and certain mental illnesses made humans return to a primitive condition. Diving into the unconscious meant a kind of backward evolution, a return to the primitive and, perhaps even worse, to the animal state. Following this theory, people who were violent were thought to be reverting to humankind's original "savage" state. In fact, much of the "evil" that had once been attributed to the work of the devil was now seen as the primitive side of humanity coming to the surface.

Such beliefs gave new meaning to old superstitions of werewolves and vampires—people who are perfectly normal at some times and real beasts at others—and it also paved the way for the notion of the "split" personality, the behavioral disorder in which different aspects of the same person are in conflict. Probably the most famous version of this dark and unsettling concept of man's hidden, primitive side is Robert Louis Stevenson's novel *The Strange Case of Dr. Jekyll and Mr. Hyde*, in which gentlemanly Dr. Jekyll discovers that "man is not truly one, but truly two." His other personality is Mr. Hyde, a savage and suitably hairy killer-ape interested only in dirty deeds.

THE MISSING LINK IS RELATED TO THE IDEA THAT MORE LINKS CAN BE ADDED

By the time Piltdown man is revealed as a hoax, scientists have turned their attention to the *Australopithecus* "ape-men," and during the 1960s that genus is finally added to the chain of human evolution: scientists come to see that it was a link missing from the chain. As a consequence, the origins of hominids are pushed back to 10, 15, even 30 million years ago.

Today, with the accumulation of discoveries of hominid fossils, the situation has changed. Fossils are no longer missing in the side of the chain leading to humans and the australopithecines; but on the side of the chimps and gorillas the fossil record is badly lacking. It is precisely there that the missing links will fit in.

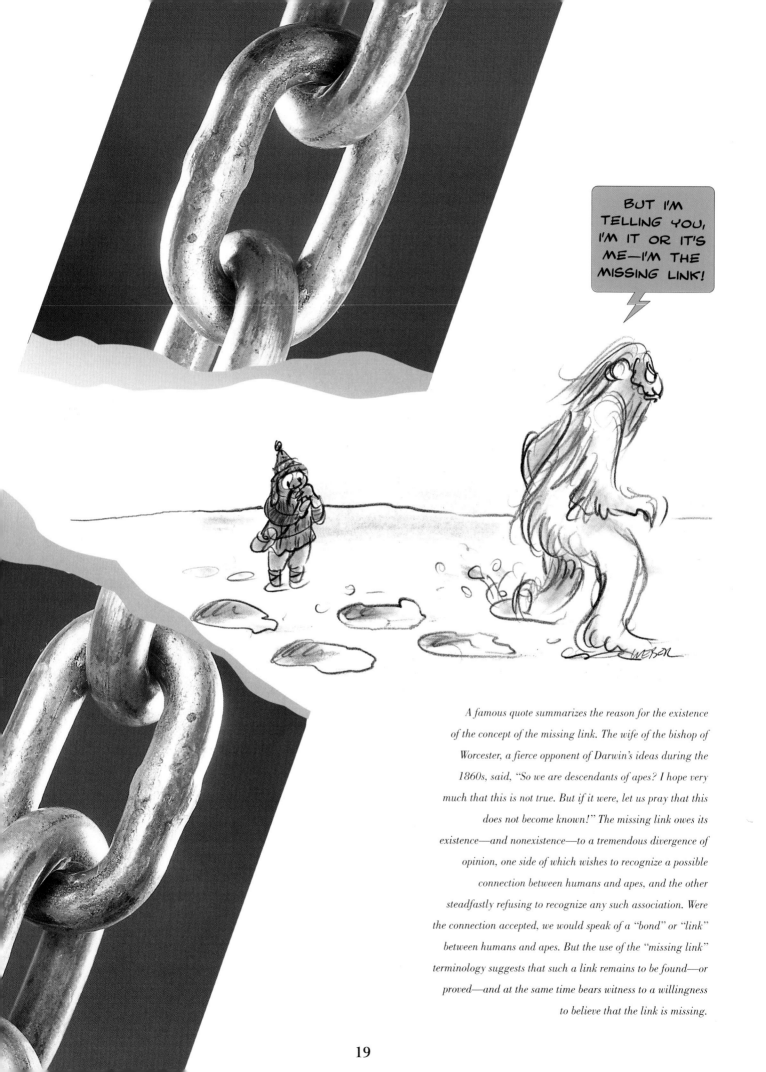

BUT I'M TELLING YOU, I'M IT OR IT'S ME—I'M THE MISSING LINK!

A famous quote summarizes the reason for the existence of the concept of the missing link. The wife of the bishop of Worcester, a fierce opponent of Darwin's ideas during the 1860s, said, "So we are descendants of apes? I hope very much that this is not true. But if it were, let us pray that this does not become known!" The missing link owes its existence—and nonexistence—to a tremendous divergence of opinion, one side of which wishes to recognize a possible connection between humans and apes, and the other steadfastly refusing to recognize any such association. Were the connection accepted, we would speak of a "bond" or "link" between humans and apes. But the use of the "missing link" terminology suggests that such a link remains to be found—or proved—and at the same time bears witness to a willingness to believe that the link is missing.

THE EVOLUTION OF EVOLUTION

Two revolutions led to evolution. The first was started by Nicholas Copernicus, who asserted that the Earth revolves around the Sun, later confirmed by the observations of Galileo Galilei. Then Isaac Newton discovered the laws of universal gravitation that govern the motion of planets. The revolutions of the stars and planets were shown to be governed by laws without the direct intervention of God.

Something similar occurred in the study of the natural world. In the oldest known texts, as well as in the Bible and other sacred works, humans are presented surrounded by the same animal and plant species known to the inhabitants of the Old World. How could anyone doubt the perfection of God's wonderful creation? The discovery of the New World made it clear that much was still to be learned about the natural world: the "unknown" plants and animals of the New World gave a great boost to scientific investigation, and the naturalists of the seventeenth and eighteenth centuries labored to catalog and classify the living beings on this planet: it seemed that the more they looked, the more they found. This work culminated in the *Systema Naturae*, by Carolus Linnaeus, in which that Swedish botanist presented the classification of plants, animals, and minerals that is the basis of today's natural sciences.

NEW IDEAS FROM THE SCIENTIFIC MIND

Other curious-minded individuals were asking questions that reached beyond the classifications. Perhaps the connections among species were the result of forces existing in nature in much the same way that gravitational forces caused the motions of the heavenly bodies. The naturalist Georges Buffon became greatly interested in the stages of Earth's development and the possible transformations of living things that had taken place. Such stages and changes required time, and Buffon estimated the Earth to be 80,000 years old, if not older. Two of the founders of geology, James Hutton and Charles Lyell, pointed out that the forces presently shaping the geography of the Earth (erosion, formation of deltas, creation of valleys) took place very slowly and had taken place just as slowly in the past. Therefore the formation of the Earth must have taken a considerable amount of time, certainly far longer than the single week mentioned in the Bible.

DARWIN'S REVOLUTION

Around the turn of the nineteenth century, several naturalists affirmed the ideas concerning the transformation of species. Jean Baptiste Lamarck presented the first coherent theory of evolution. He recognized that many ancient species had not died out but had changed (evolved) into the species of today; he believed that living things progressed from simple to more complex forms and that they adapted to changes in environment or behavior. Giraffes, for example, developed long necks as a result of continually stretching to feed on high tree branches. In short, function creates an organ, and such acquired characteristics (like the long neck) are passed on to descendants. Lamarck believed that such transformations resulted from the active interaction between an individual and the environment. His theory of acquired characteristics was savagely criticized by many, but the second revolution was on its way, and it exploded when Darwin showed that all species have evolved by means of natural selection and that humans ultimately descend from apes.

SIGMUND FREUD (1856-1939)
"Over the centuries humanity has had to endure great outrages upon its naive self-love. First, when it realized that our Earth was not the center of the universe, but only a speck in a world-system of a magnitude hardly conceivable; and second, when biology robbed man of his particular privilege of having been specially created, and relegated him to descent from the animal world."

NICHOLAS COPERNICUS (1473-1543)
Through his calculations he demonstrated that it is not the Sun that revolves around the Earth (geocentrism) but rather the Earth that revolves around the Sun (heliocentrism).

GALILEO GALILEI (1564-1642)
He invented the first astronomical telescope, which enabled him to observe the motions of the planets and to confirm the theories of Copernicus.

CAROLUS LINNAEUS (1707-78)
Founder of the binomial system of nomenclature and originator of modern scientific classification of plants and animals. He classified man among the primates.

GEORGES BUFFON (1707-88)
He dedicated his life to a monumental work on natural history and investigated the forces that connect species. He believed that species can change and suggested that the Earth is very old.

JAMES HUTTON (1726-97)
One of the founders of geology. He believed that Earth's history can be explained by observing the geological forces now at work, since they are the same as those of the past.

JEAN BAPTISTE LAMARCK (1744-1829)
He proposed a theory of evolution (Lamarckism) according to which all life forms are the result of a continuous process of gradual modification; he introduced the term *biology* and is considered the founder of invertebrate paleontology.

GEORGES CUVIER (1769-1832)
A pioneer in the sciences of comparative anatomy and paleontology, he rejected the theory of evolution in favor of catastrophism, the doctrine that claimed animal fossils are the result of periodic floods and earthquakes.

ALFRED RUSSEL WALLACE (1823-1913)
He stated the principle of natural selection simultaneously with Darwin, in 1858. He coined the term *Darwinism* and affirmed that natural selection is the only driving force of evolution.

THOMAS HUXLEY (1825-95)
Friend and fierce defender of Darwin. He wrote a book about the place of humans in nature that demonstrated the great resemblance between humans and the great apes.

THE LIFE OF DARWIN

*Charles Darwin is born in 1809 in a
well-to-do family of liberal ideas. His
grandfather Erasmus Darwin already
has evolutionist ideas. Young Charles
is only an average student and
abandons his medical studies at
Edinburgh, deciding to move to
Cambridge and become a pastor.
Under the tutelage of the botanist John
Stevens Henslow, he develops a great
passion for nature. It is Henslow who
sets Darwin on his path toward destiny
when he urges the young man to join
the crew of the* Beagle *as naturalist.
The five-year voyage brings back to
England a person brimming with
evolutionist ideas. He marries his
cousin Emma Wedgwood and then,
because of his fragile health, moves in
1842 to a residence in the country,
Down House, about 16 miles south of
London. There he composes his major
work,* On the Origin of Species by
Means of Natural Selection, *which is
published in 1859. What a huge
scandal! However, "the most
dangerous man in England"—as
Darwin is labeled by Bishop Samuel
Wilberforce—ultimately triumphs, and
when he dies in 1882 he is buried in
Westminster Abbey alongside Newton.*

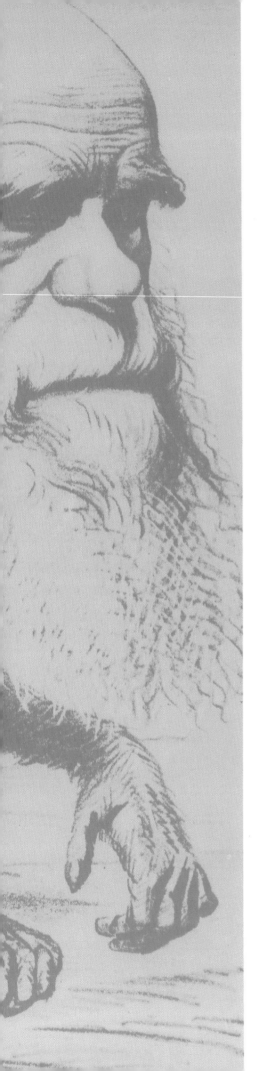

THE MOST DANGEROUS MAN IN ENGLAND

In 1831 a twenty-one-year-old naturalist embarks on the *Beagle* for a five-year voyage to South America. He is Charles Darwin. During the trip he gathers specimens, keeps careful journals, and makes important observations. For example, he notices that extinct species of armadillos resemble species living today. He also notes that populations of the same species, such as ostriches, gradually change from one region to another to the extent that there are significant differences between populations at the far ends of the South American continent. He observes that the finches on the Galapagos Islands have characteristics that differ from those of the original population, which came from the mainland. It is clear to him that some form of evolution has taken place, with physical characteristics being transformed in time and space to give birth to a new species. Let's see how it happened.

THE SURVIVAL OF THE FITTEST

Darwin is particularly interested in the work of breeders, who create special varieties of wheat or breeds of dog, for example, by crossing specimens that have desirable characteristics. Breeders have a goal in mind, of course, and such is not the case in nature. Then Darwin reads an essay on population by Thomas Malthus stating that all creatures, including humans, produce more offspring than available resources can support; this situation leads to wars and famines. Darwin applies Malthus's idea to nature. Here, too, Darwin contends, far too many individuals are born in each generation for the resources available. Consequently, the natural world is the stage for competition.

By definition, each individual differs from the next: some individuals have characteristics that give them an edge in gaining access to food, to better shelter, and to mating partners. It's these "more fit" individuals who survive. They are able to reproduce and transmit their characteristics to their offspring: this is natural selection. It is the mechanism that causes evolution, which is brought about by the accumulation of these changes from one generation to the next.

This type of slow and gradual evolution through natural selection is called the Darwinian process. Over time, certain species become extinct while others come into being and multiply; all are connected somewhere in the history of life by common ancestors. Evolutionary lines are like the branches of a tree that become longer, intertwine, regress, or disappear in time. The presentation of the mechanism of natural selection is Darwin's greatest contribution. All the elements of his theory are published in 1859 in the work entitled *On the Origin of Species*. In his works, Darwin doesn't say that humans are descended from apes or monkeys, but even so people soon understand that "man descended from apes."

A FOSSIL'S LIFE IS A VERY HARD LIFE

TO BE OR NOT TO BE . . . AND TO BE AGAIN

THE TERM *FOSSIL* COMES FROM THE LATIN *FOSSILIS*, MEANING "DUG UP." FOSSILS ARE REMAINS OF ORGANISMS PRESERVED IN SEDIMENTARY DEPOSITS. TO WHAT EXTENT DID THEY CONTRIBUTE TO THE FORMULATION OF THE THEORY OF EVOLUTION?

FOSSILS: THE EARLY DAYS

References to the remains of vanished animals date back to earliest antiquity, but only during the eighteenth century do naturalists begin to look at fossils with scientific curiosity. Until then, some people think fossils represent animals that lived before the biblical flood and happened to "miss the boat" with Noah's ark; others think fossils are remains of animals still living in remote regions of the world. But as increasingly strange fossil forms are discovered, and as the far corners of the world are opened to human exploration, such theories lose their force. Georges Cuvier explains it all with his theory of catastrophism, according to which all living things have periodically been destroyed by natural disasters. According to Cuvier, all the species remain unchanged from catastrophe to catastrophe. He fiercely opposes the very notion of evolution, particularly the kind of changes proposed by Jean Baptiste Lamarck.

THE THEORY OF EVOLUTION GIVES LIFE TO FOSSILS

Charles Darwin dedicates only one of the fifteen chapters in his *Origin of Species* to fossils, for his demonstration of the evolution of species by means of natural selection relies essentially on the study of living organisms. However, fossils are presented as proof of evolution. This does not mean that the fossils discovered by the young Charles Darwin did not contribute to the formulation of his theory, but they do not represent the foundation of his demonstration. But while fossils did not forge the theory of evolution, the theory of evolution revealed the enormous importance of fossils. If living organisms are related by kinship, then the fossil record should contain intermediary fossil forms of distant relatives.

Today the study of the "life" of fossils is a separate science. In order to reconstruct the past it is important to understand the natural conditions leading to fossilization. In fact, an organism will be well preserved if it is buried rapidly. Water offers good conditions for this to occur. No wonder most of the hominoid remains have been found in ancient aquatic environments (alluvial plains, river banks, marshes). Forests are not at all favorable to fossilization since bones are not well preserved in acidic soil. And speaking of bones, it's usually only the hard parts of a creature that become fossilized, so determining what an extinct being looked like "in the flesh" can be difficult.

Alas, poor Lucy! I knew her.

WHERE THE PIECES FIT

1. *occipital (AL 288-1a)*
2. *l. parietal (AL 288-1b)*
3. *l. parieto-frontal (AL 288-1c,g)*
4. *r. parietal (AL 288-1e)*
5. *r. frontal (AL 288-1h)*
6. *mandible (AL 288-1i,j,k)*
7. *l. humerus (AL 288-1r,s)*
8. *l. ulna (AL 288-1t,u)*
9. *l. radius (AL 288-1v)*
10. *bone of the l. wrist (AL 288-1w)*
11. *phalanx of l. hand (AL 288-1y)*
12. *r. scapula (AL 288-1l)*
13. *r. humerus (AL 288-1m)*
14. *r. ulna (AL 288-1n,o)*
15. *r. radius (AL 288-1p,q)*
16. *sacrum (AL 288-1an)*
17. *l. ilium (wing of the hip) (AL 288-1ao)*
18. *l. femur (AL 288-1ap)*
19. *r. tibia (AL 288-1aq,ar)*
20. *r. fibula (AL 288-1at)*
21. *r. talus (AL 288-1as)*
22. *1st phalanx r. foot (AL 288- 1y)*
23. *2nd phalanx r. foot (AL 288-1z)*

24.
to   *thoracic vertebrae*
30.   *(AL 288-1ac to AL 288-1ag)*

31. *lumbar vertebrae (AL 288-1aa,ak,al)*

32.
to   *fragments of ribs*
42.   *(AL 288-1au to AL 288-1bz)*

l. = left; r. = right

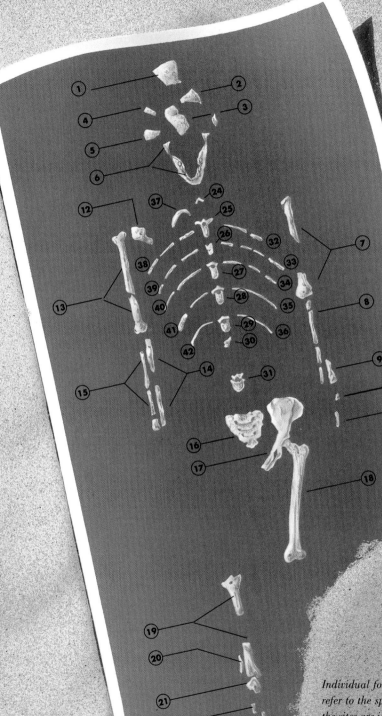

NAMING FOSSILS

Individual fossils are designated by codes that refer to the specific site where they were found; the sites are identified by codes composed of letters and numbers. AL 288, for example, stands for "Afar Locality, number 288." The fossils found at each site are further coded according to the order in which they are collected. The codename for Lucy's site is AL 288-1; the 78 bone fragments were listed using the alphabet, repeating and combining letters as needed: AL 288-1a, AL 288-1b and on to AL 288-1z: then AL 288-1ab and so on to AL 288-1bz.

BONE RUSH

THE TOOLS MAKE THE HOMINID

It's not until 1959 that australopithecines "officially" enter the hominid family. The place: Olduvai Gorge in East Africa. On a pleasant morning, Mary Leakey discovers a magnificent robust australopithecine skull buried next to some tools. Since at that time only humans and their ancestors were believed to have made tools, the "indirect proof" offered by the tools—and not the physical appearance of the species—serves to win the australopithecines their hominid certificate. Since then, everyone's attention has centered on Africa.

HUMANS IN THE LAND OF THE AUSTRALOPITHECINES

The discovery touches off a veritable "bone rush," and many excavation campaigns are launched: the Omo Research Expedition (Camille Arambourg, Yves Coppens, and Francis Clark Howell), the Turkana Lake Project (Koobi Fora Research Project—Richard, followed by Meave Leakey), the Middle Awash Valley Project (Jon Kalb), Louis and Mary Leakey at Olduvai Gorge, and later Mary Leakey at Laetoli. This is the area that the geologist Maurice Taïeb explores during the late 1960s. Interested in the formation of the Awash River in the Afar Triangle of Ethiopia, he estimates that the geological formations are about 3 million years old. In cooperation with Yves Coppens, Donald Johanson, and Jon Kalb, he launches the International Afar Research Expedition (IARE). In 1973, the members of the French-American-Ethiopian team index 89 localities that contain fossils and find a hominid knee. Then, finally, on a November day in 1974, they come across bone fragments that constitute 40 percent of the skeleton of a small australopithecine, which they name Lucy. During four excavation campaigns IARE brings to light a total of 240 hominid fossils belonging to some thirty specimens. This proves to be paleoanthropology's most fruitful expedition ever.

There are no campaigns in Ethiopia between 1977 and 1990, then research is resumed by various international teams. A splendid male skull is found in 1992, twenty years after Lucy. And even more recently, fossils more ancient than Lucy—those of *Ardipithecus ramidus*—are unearthed. The adventure continues . . .

CALENDAR OF EVENTS FOR THE INTERNATIONAL AFAR RESEARCH EXPEDITION (IARE)

1972: IARE is created by Yves Coppens, Donald Johanson, Jon Kalb, and Maurice Taïeb.
1973: Discovery of a knee joint.
1974: Discovery of Lucy.
1975: Discovery of the remains of thirteen individuals at site AL 333—the "first family."
1976-77: Discovery of other fossils at site AL 333 and elsewhere.

No sooner has Lucy been lifted out of her cradle of sediment than various people begin seeing different things in her. What they see depends on their scientific inclination. Some see her as an early *Homo*; some say she's an ape; others think she's an australopithecine but can't decide whether she's gracile or robust. The problem is, now that we've found Lucy, how do we classify her? One thing is certain, though: Lucy definitely has star power.

PART HARMONY

The members of the International Afar Research Expedition do without many comforts, but not their tape player; this is 1974, and they're particularly fond of the Beatles. A popular song in camp is "Lucy in the Sky with Diamonds," and thus the name Lucy comes to mind for the new species of human predecessor. Only after you're named can you properly be introduced. Lucy's introduction to "high society" comes in three parts.

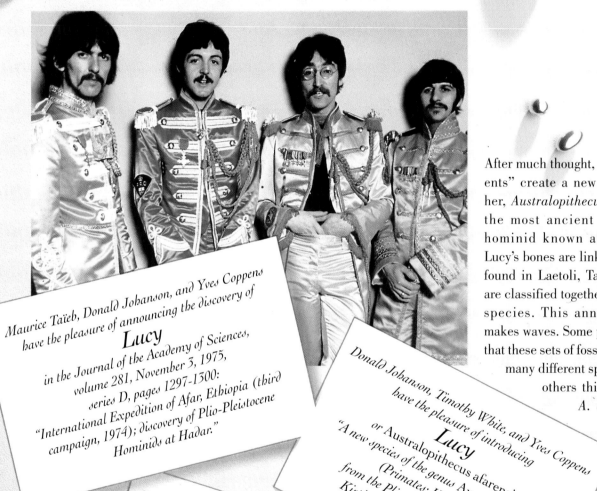

Maurice Taïeb, Donald Johanson, and Yves Coppens have the pleasure of announcing the discovery of

Lucy

in the Journal of the Academy of Sciences, volume 281, November 3, 1975, series D, pages 1297-1300: "International Expedition of Afar, Ethiopia (third campaign, 1974); discovery of Plio-Pleistocene Hominids at Hadar."

Donald Johanson, Timothy White, and Yves Coppens have the pleasure of introducing

Lucy

or Australopithecus afarensis: "A new species of the genus Australopithecus (Primates: Hominidae) from the Pliocene of Eastern Africa." Kirtlandia 28 (1978), pages 1-14.

Donald Johanson, Maurice Taïeb, Yves Coppens, Tim D. White, and friends invite you to discover

Lucy

in a special volume of the American Journal of Physical Anthropology, no. 57 (4), April 1982: "Pliocene Hominid Fossils from Hadar, Ethiopia."

1

In the first announcement Lucy is introduced along with the other fossils from the site at Hadar. She is described as being similar to the gracile australopithecines of South Africa. But some of her bones seem more connected to the robust australopithecines or to early humans. In any case, Lucy's proud "parents" let the world in on their discovery.

2

After much thought, Lucy's "parents" create a new species for her, *Australopithecus afarensis*, the most ancient species of hominid known at the time. Lucy's bones are linked to others found in Laetoli, Tanzania, and are classified together in a single species. This announcement makes waves. Some people think that these sets of fossils represent many different species, while others think that this *A. afarensis* is nothing more than a regional variant of *A. africanus* of South Africa.

3

Lucy and her kin are finally "properly" introduced to the public at large. All of them are described and photographed. But the debate goes on concerning the true meaning of the species *Australopithecus afarensis*. Lucy finds herself at center stage in an international anthropological squabble. Celebrities are always controversial.

HAPPY BIRTHDAY, LUCY!

*How old am I?
You'll have to figure that
out yourself.
Go ahead, guess.*

RIFT CAKE

The Earth's continents are slowly moving; this geological fact is quite evident in Africa, where a fault line known as the Great Rift Valley runs from Ethiopia in the north to Malawi in the south: about 50 million years from now the right side of this line may break away to form a new continent. In the regions of the Great Rift, including the Afar Triangle, the crust of the Earth has been pushed up and exposed like a big layer cake, and those layers of ancient sediment whet the appetite of geologists in much the same way that a cake appeals to any birthday girl (or boy).

TELLING TIME WITH DIRT

Some of the exposed geological layers contain volcanic ash (tuff). This tuff bears crystals laden with potassium, a chemical element that slowly changes into argon through nuclear transmutation. Since scientists know how long it takes for this change to take place, they use that number to calculate the age of each geological layer. So, thanks to volcanoes, precise ages can be assigned to the various layers of the terrestrial "cake." Even so, this method is accurate only for older layers—those formed at least 100,000 years ago. Other methods of dating use similar natural phenomena. It has been determined that Lucy was wedged between two layers of volcanic tuff, one dating to 3.18 million years ago, the other 2.9 million years ago.

NORTH IS NORTH, RIGHT?

Scientists have determined that the Earth's "north" has reversed itself at regular intervals throughout the planet's history. During such periods, instead of pointing toward the North Pole to indicate magnetic north, the needle of a compass points instead toward the South Pole. These inversions in the planet's magnetic field are clearly recorded in the Earth's rocks because they all contain iron. When fine particles of magnetized iron deposit slowly, as they do in calm water, they line up according to the direction of the magnetic field of that particular time. Lucy was found in a layer resting between two layers of reversed magnetic "icing" named Kaena and Mammoth.

WHAT THE ANIMALS SAY

The evolution of pigs, elephants, horses, and several other animals has been well documented by paleoanthropologists throughout the geological layers. Finding a fossil of one of those animals in a layer of sediment enables scientists to date the layer and thus any other fossils found there, such as those of early humans. All these dating systems help scientists determine the age of our ancestors, including that of dear "old" Lucy. With a birthday cake it's easy enough to figure out the age: all you have to do is count the candles. With fossils, it's just a bit trickier.

WHAT'S THE DATE OF HADAR?

Scientists divide geological layers into various sections, which are then given names. The layers containing tuff are important because they can be dated; the various layers at Hadar are named according to the tuff associated with them. Lucy's layer of the Hadar formation dates to the period of normal magnetism known as the Gauss period, namely between 3.3 and 2.4 million years ago.

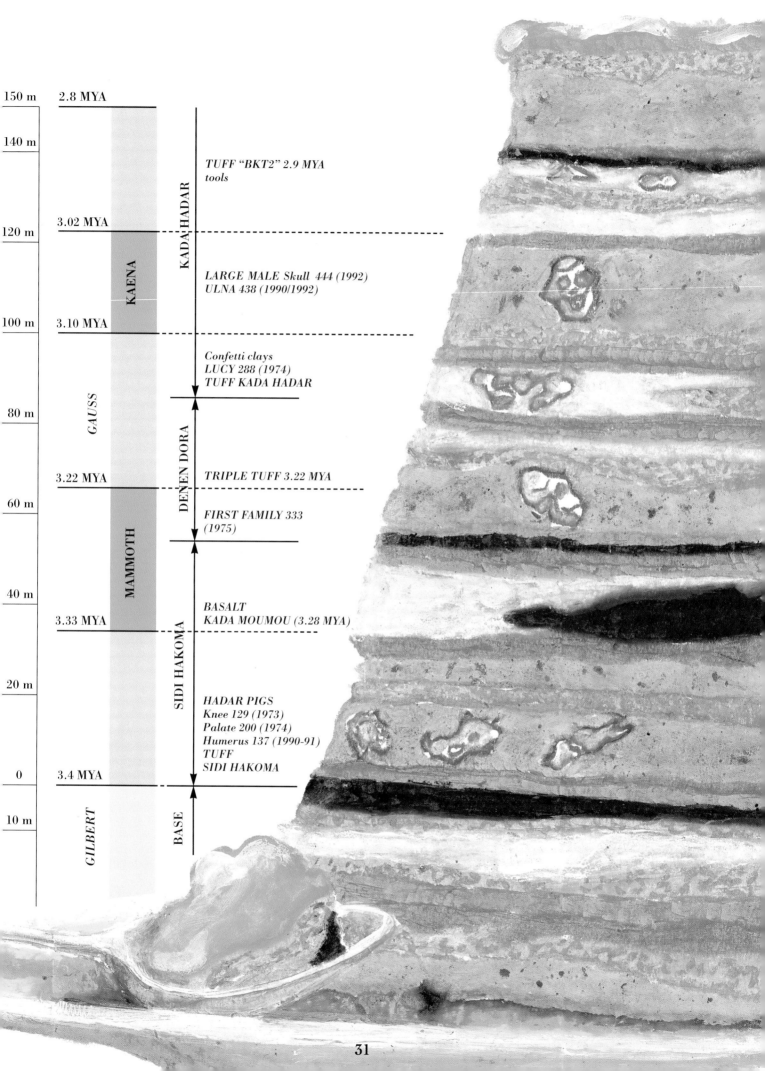

150 m	2.8 MYA			
140 m				
				TUFF "BKT2" 2.9 MYA *tools*
120 m	3.02 MYA		KADA HADAR	
		KAENA		*LARGE MALE Skull 444 (1992)* *ULNA 438 (1990/1992)*
100 m	3.10 MYA			
	GAUSS		DENEN DORA	*Confetti clays* *LUCY 288 (1974)* *TUFF KADA HADAR*
80 m				
				TRIPLE TUFF 3.22 MYA
60 m	3.22 MYA	MAMMOTH		*FIRST FAMILY 333* *(1975)*
40 m			SIDI HAKOMA	*BASALT* *KADA MOUMOU (3.28 MYA)*
20 m	3.33 MYA			
				HADAR PIGS *Knee 129 (1973)* *Palate 200 (1974)* *Humerus 137 (1990-91)* *TUFF* *SIDI HAKOMA*
0	3.4 MYA			
10 m		GILBERT	BASE	

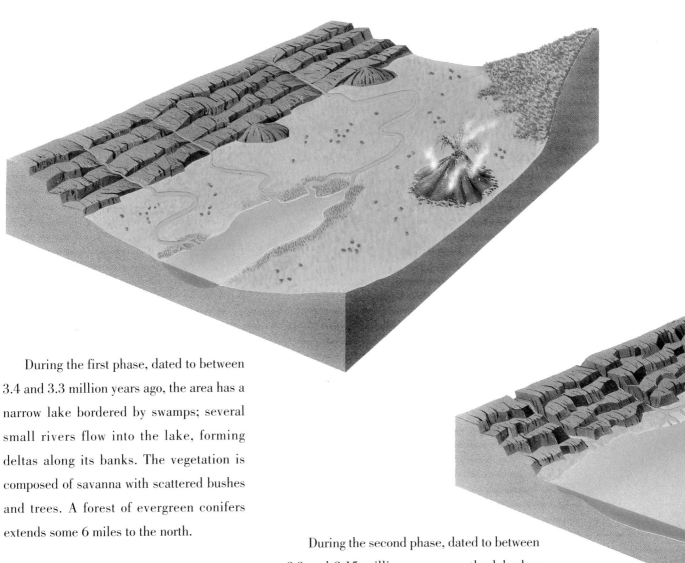

During the first phase, dated to between 3.4 and 3.3 million years ago, the area has a narrow lake bordered by swamps; several small rivers flow into the lake, forming deltas along its banks. The vegetation is composed of savanna with scattered bushes and trees. A forest of evergreen conifers extends some 6 miles to the north.

During the second phase, dated to between 3.3 and 3.15 million years ago, the lake has greatly expanded. The climate is drier. The surrounding vegetation is composed of more open savannas, with wild grasses, and the conifer forest to the north has nearly vanished.

The savanna of Lucy's time

CHANGES, LIFE CHANGES

WARNING: FALLING LANDSCAPE ZONE

The Hadar formation is located in the Afar Triangle of Ethiopia. This region north of the Great Rift Valley has undergone important geological changes that altered the course of rivers and the size of lakes. During Lucy's time, Hadar was at an altitude of more than 3,000 feet. The collapse of the Afar Triangle made it drop more than 1,600 feet. The landscape was far lusher than it is today, and the animal life of Hadar was dominated by species like the impala, which prefer woodland savannas. The vast garden in which Lucy lived consisted of a mosaic of sparse forests growing near water and vast woodland savannas and wide patches covered with wild grasses. In fewer than 500,000 years, this landscape goes through the three phases shown here.

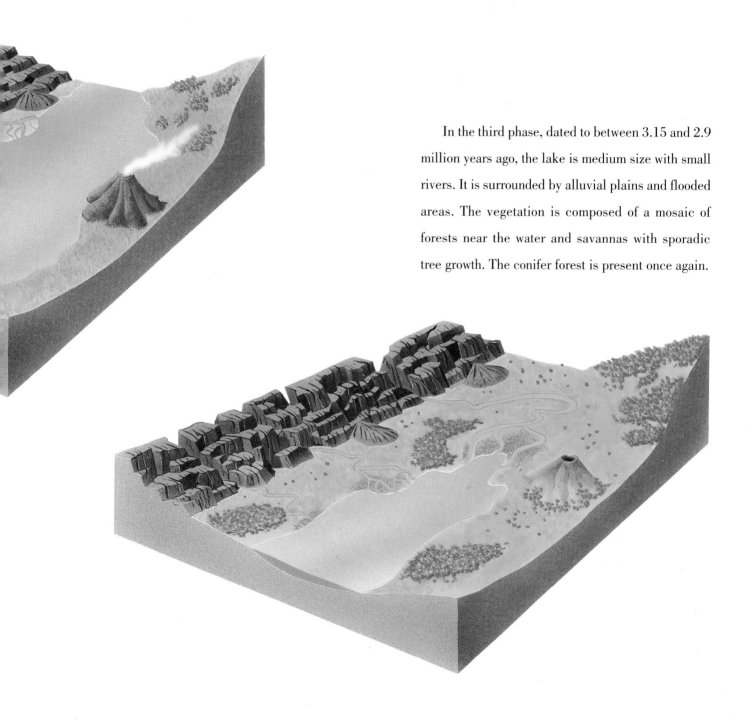

In the third phase, dated to between 3.15 and 2.9 million years ago, the lake is medium size with small rivers. It is surrounded by alluvial plains and flooded areas. The vegetation is composed of a mosaic of forests near the water and savannas with sporadic tree growth. The conifer forest is present once again.

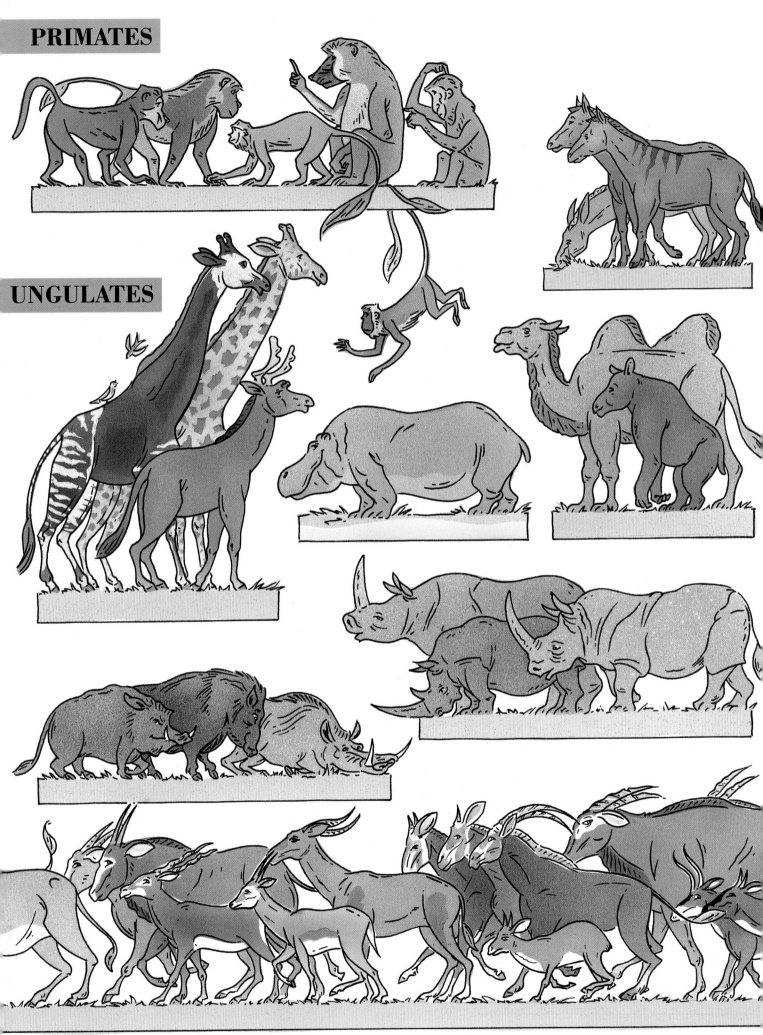

CARNIVORES

PROBOSCIDEANS

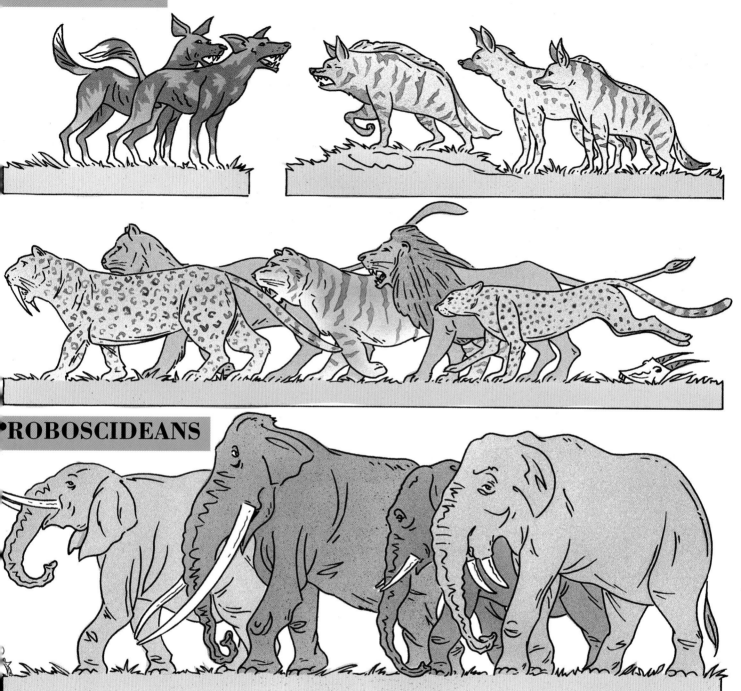

IT'S CROWDED ON THE SAVANNA!

The wildlife of Lucy's time was similar to that of today, but the animals were much more exotic and diversified. They are known today as the Ethiopian fauna. The coming of the savannas brought about the golden age of the Bovidae (the antelope family, which includes antelopes, gazelles, and oxen). The landscape was crowded with large species of mammals, but the panorama was not without birds and reptiles. With so many animals it seems possible that there may also have been numerous species of hominids, contemporaries of Lucy, including early humans and the australopithecines of Kenya. All the animal species presented here were common to the period between 4 and 3 million years ago, and alongside them may have been many hominids. This diversity was to vanish during the ice ages.

The Bible was often used to explain the various stages of evolution. In fact, until the nineteenth century the story of Noah's ark was frequently cited in attempts to explain the disappearance of animals known only from fossils; such creatures were thought to have lived before the flood and shown up late for the ark—they never got on board.

The biblical story was also used to explain the distribution of animals. Thus some species or groups of species are found only in one place because that was their "home port"—that was where they headed after the waters receded. Noah's ark thus served to explain why some animals no longer exist and why certain animals are found only in certain areas of the world.

WHAT ABOUT THE ANIMALS THAT MISSED THE BOAT?

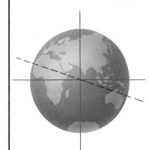
THE WANDERINGS OF THE HOMINOIDS

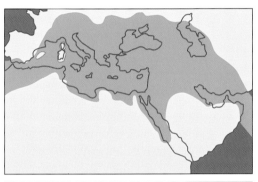

A PARADISE IN AFRICA
The period between 20 and 17 million years ago is the golden age of our hominoid ancestors in East Africa. The region of Africa is a paradise separated from the other continents by the ancient Tethys Sea.

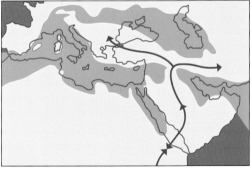

FAREWELL, AFRICA
The climate becomes drier, and the hominoids disappear from the region. A group migrates to Eurasia around 15.5 million years ago, taking advantage of an opening across the Tethys Sea.

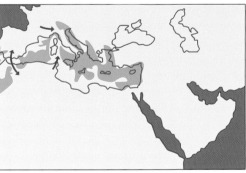

THE DELIGHTS OF EURASIA
Between 15 and 8 million years ago the southern fringes of Eurasia are covered with vast forests in which the hominoids prosper. But the weather deteriorates, and the delights of Eurasia eventually turn into a curse.

THE IMPOSSIBLE RETURN

While the hominoids were living mainly in Eurasia, could a group of them have succeeded in returning to Africa and thus initiating another expansion, that of the hominids, around 7 million years ago? Was there a "Noah's ark" chartered for a trip from Eurasia to Africa? This seems quite unlikely since at that time the Mediterranean Sea was dried and the regions around it were deprived of forests, and the hominoids depended on trees for survival. In fact, it is thought that some hominoids, ancestors of the hominids and of Lucy, remained in Africa between 15 and 8 million years ago, but they have not been discovered so far.

STORM WARNING:
ICE AGES ARE COMING

THE EARTH'S DANCE AROUND THE SUN

The Earth rotates around the Sun, but with some regular peculiarities that have immense consequences on the climate. First of all, the Earth doesn't rotate in a circular orbit. Its head is more or less tilted, so its orbit is elliptical. Second, it behaves like a toy top that revolves steadily. This funny dance regulates how much heat the Earth receives from the Sun. This produces glacial periods, which have been occurring regularly every 500,000 years ever since around 10 million years ago. These ice ages have caused repeated droughts in Africa.

THE CONTINENTS DANCE, TOO

On Earth, the continents continuously fidget, especially Africa, which seems to be constantly on the move. By moving up toward the north, it has contributed to the formation of the Mediterranean Sea, but it also cut it off by closing the Strait of Gibraltar around 6 million years ago. You can probably imagine the effects this had on the climate! No Club Med, especially for the hominids. Africa is breaking into pieces, and the Rift valleys are actually a developing ocean. The spurs of the Rift rise and give birth to high plateaus that block the circulation of clouds and thus have an impact on the climate.

The weather was more pleasant during Lucy's time, but it eventually deteriorated, leading to an ice age that lasted for millions of years (and it may have seemed even longer).

Lucy got her name from a Beatles song, but the name Lucy turns out to be well-suited for someone from the "dawn" of humanity. *Lucy* comes from a Latin word meaning "light"—in fact, the ancient Romans used the name for girls born early in the morning. And in a broader sense, the discovery of Lucy has shed light on what we know of the past. Essential to understanding Lucy's world is understanding the importance of weather (as in whether or not the sun will shine).

KNOWING THE WEATHER

POLLEN ADVISORY

Plants reproduce by means of grains of pollen that are spread by the wind or by animals like birds and insects. Each plant has a different kind of pollen, and since pollen fossilizes well today's scientists know much about the plants of the past. The pollen found in Hadar indicates that there was an evergreen conifer forest in the neighborhood. Other pollen from trees and plants suggests a relatively dry savanna environment with acacias, bushes, and grasses. The forests grew thicker around rivers and lakes. This must have provided a beautiful landscape for Lucy to live in.

NEWS FROM THE IMPALAS

The expansion of the savannas in East Africa created a true paradise for the Bovidae family of mammals. Among these are the African antelopes known as impalas, which prefer heavily wooded zones where they can feed at will on the abundant leaves of trees and bushes; gazelles prefer drier zones where they can graze on grass or the leaves of bushes. Fossil remains indicate that at Hadar, between 3.5 and 3 million years ago, there were far more impalas than gazelles, a factor indicating an environment of a savanna with trees.

READING WEATHER IN DIRT

The ground is the skin of the Earth. Its state is directly effected by climate and by the plants and animals living on it. The fossilized soil of site AL 333 of Hadar contains sand, clay, and sandstone, a situation that suggests a flooded plain in the vicinity of a river. The amount of annual rainfall must have been relatively small: approximately 20 to 32 inches of water per year, which fell during one or two seasons. Traces of roots indicate plants growing on a savanna with acacia trees. Grasses were abundant and quite tall (around three feet high). This information leads scientists to believe that Lucy's climate was relatively dry, with temperatures ranging from 64 to 72 degrees in January and between 88 and 99 degrees in July.

YESTERDAY'S (6 MILLION YEARS AGO) WEATHER REPORT

Between 6 and 4.5 million years ago, the climate was somewhat more humid in Afar than it is today. Then, between 4.3 and 3 million years ago, the world's glaciers began melting and thus holding less water: the climate became more humid throughout Africa, particularly during Lucy's time. But the long-range weather forecast would have been gloomy. The situation became worse around 2.5 million years ago, when the Arctic icecap joined the ice sheets of North America and northern Europe: a truly big chill. As a result, the australopithecines from Afar as well as most of the gracile australopithecines vanished. The robust australopithecines and early humans took advantage of these circumstances to flourish. But then another cold wave struck around 1 million years ago and proved fatal to the robust australopithecines, leaving only the all-weather humans. Needless to say, this also meant curtains for much of the Ethiopian fauna.

THE FOREST

West of the Rift Valley the populations of a common ancestor will evolve toward today's anthropoid, or manlike, apes (chimpanzees, bonobo chimps, and gorillas). Their evolution is linked to that of the forest environment on which they strongly depend. As of now we know nothing about the physical appearance of our common ancestor, but one thing is sure: it didn't look anything like the big African apes of today. These are very specialized in their quadruped mode of locomotion.

EAST SIDE STORY

GEOGRAPHY GOES HAND IN HAND WITH CLIMATE

Once upon a time there was a big, beautiful forest that extended from one side of Africa to the other, from the Gulf of Guinea in the west to the shores of Mombasa in the east. So begins Yves Coppens' own "East Side Story," which reconstructs the origin of the hominids. Around 8 million years ago, Africa shifts again. The Rift valleys and their spurs become greatly distorted, with growing hollows and high plateaus. This geographical barrier quickly becomes a climatic one. The west, always watered by rains from the Gulf of Guinea, maintains its tropical forests. The annual rainfall is above 75 inches, with a rainy season that lasts ten months. These rains do not extend to the east, however, and that region is subjected to a more seasonal climate based on the rhythm of the monsoons from the Indian Ocean. The landscape changes, offering patches of forest along lakes and river banks and creating forested savannas. With annual rainfall around 40 inches, the savannas preserve some of their trees. But without 20 to 40 inches per year the savannas become wide open fields ruthlessly besieged by dry periods lasting many months.

THE SAVANNA

The environment does not change at once east of the Great Rift Valley. The zones with trees have been progressively penetrated by grassy areas. The first hominids depend on trees for their survival (food, shelter, protection against predators). Lucy spends as much time in the trees as she does on the ground among the impalas. Only later, around 3 million years ago, do certain hominids venture into open ground, attracted by the new horizons freed from the clutches of the glaciers.

APES: THEY COME AND GO WITH

For more than 20 million years, the immense African tropical forest plays a tune that the apes sometimes have difficulty following. Africa dances to the rhythm of the ice ages, but its inhabitants often miss a step. At different times the forests expand or contract, and the contractions force various groups of large and small primates to adapt to more open environments. This is the case with the hominids, who remain east of the Rift Valley beginning around 7 million years ago. But soon they spread out around the big forests, as indicated by the presence of australopithecines in Chad (Abel), in South Africa (*A. africanus*), and, of course, in East Africa. They share the woodland savannas with formidable and fearsome apes.

3 MILLION YEARS AGO
Hominids live all around the tropical forest. They are found side by side with the monkeys of the more open environments, such as the geladas and baboons. Were those forests also home to ancestors of today's baboons and even of the hominids? We don't know, because the forest environment is not favorable to the preservation of fossils.

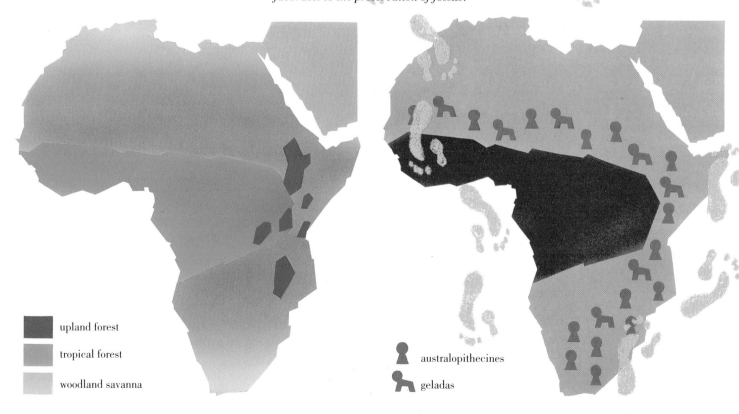

upland forest

tropical forest

woodland savanna

australopithecines

geladas

THE RHYTHM OF THE ICE AGES

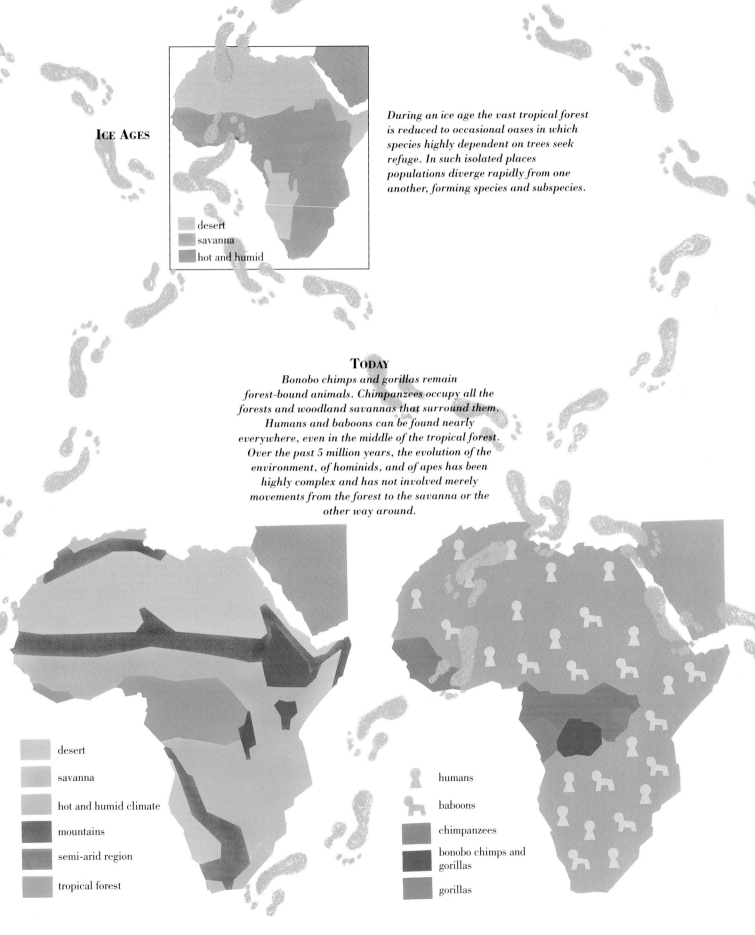

ICE AGES

desert
savanna
hot and humid

During an ice age the vast tropical forest is reduced to occasional oases in which species highly dependent on trees seek refuge. In such isolated places populations diverge rapidly from one another, forming species and subspecies.

TODAY
Bonobo chimps and gorillas remain forest-bound animals. Chimpanzees occupy all the forests and woodland savannas that surround them. Humans and baboons can be found nearly everywhere, even in the middle of the tropical forest. Over the past 5 million years, the evolution of the environment, of hominids, and of apes has been highly complex and has not involved merely movements from the forest to the savanna or the other way around.

desert
savanna
hot and humid climate
mountains
semi-arid region
tropical forest

humans
baboons
chimpanzees
bonobo chimps and gorillas
gorillas

45

MR. BY-THE-BOOK

3

On the savannas the first hominids learned to use tools and began living in social groups. The males in each group protected the group. The males were monogamous and hunted meat for the females; in exchange, the females gave them their favors and fidelity.

4

Between 5 and 3 million years ago these first hominids constitute a common parent-stock that includes various subspecies of gracile australopithecines. Later, around 2.5 million years ago, this common stock divides into two large lineages: one is the robust australopithecines (Paranthropus) and the other is the early humans (Homo).

5

Hominization describes in concrete terms the long march of evolution from ape to humans. Bipedalism led to the liberation of the hands, and the interaction of hands, tools, and brain has ensured the appearance of a thinking human species.

2

The most ancient hominids originated in East Africa. This verifies two of Darwin's predictions: that Africa would prove to be the cradle of humanity and that bipedalism must have evolved as an adaptation to life on the savanna.

1

The evolutionary history of the hominids can be reconstructed on the basis of the data that has been assembled thus far combined with the simplest models of hominization.

THE DEVIL'S ADVOCATE

3

Here we go again! From apes to angels by way of a tool kit! Lucy sure used her teeth a lot, munching throughout her life. So much for tools. As for the fruits of passion, she didn't have to bother with just one male; monogamy, fidelity, and reproduction tell quite a different story when seen from the devil's angle.

4

That's a real hoot. First of all, the australopithecines from Afar were not alone at that time. And, to be honest, it's not definite that they were indeed our ancestors. Early humans may have been already roaming around 3 million years ago, along with other australopithecines. Their kinship is even more complicated than the jagged teeth of my pitchfork.

5

When you're the only species left, it's easy to gloat. To the victor go the spoils, and the brains. Why don't we ask the baboons for their version of evolution? It might be amusing to learn all about the process of baboonization.

2

Indeed. But given the promising new discoveries that are beginning to emerge in South and West Africa, hard times may be in store for paleoanthropologists. After all, this history of bipedalism and the savanna is just a bit too simple, even if it was Darwin who dreamed it up. Remember, baboons are quadrupeds from the same region, and they get along quite well, too.

1

Obviously! But that's only part of the story. If Michel Brunet and Yves Coppens had stuck by Mr. Coppens' "East Side Story," Abel would never have been found.

FOR PURPOSES OF COMPARISON, DO NOT CROSS THIS LINE

3.5 ft.

PYGMY   **CHIMPANZEE**   **GIRL**   **LUCY**

Lucy was small. Everyone agrees about that. But she was by no means a miniature female of her species. In other words, th

various parts of her body cannot be compared to the body of a small woman, the way a Barbie doll or toy soldier is in scale with

real, full-grown human. The best way to understand Lucy's body size is to compare it to the bodies of similar individuals of the sam

size. We have compared Lucy with a pygmy woman, a female chimp, and a nine-year-old girl. Many of the differences are obviou

aren't they?

THINGS UP

TELL ME, DOCTOR, WHAT DO THE X-RAYS SHOW?

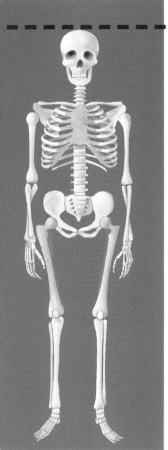
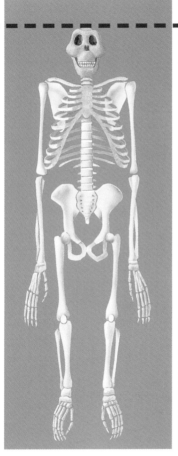
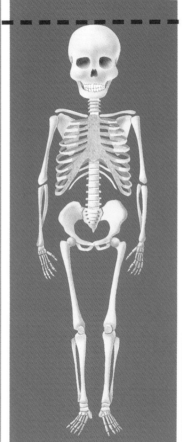
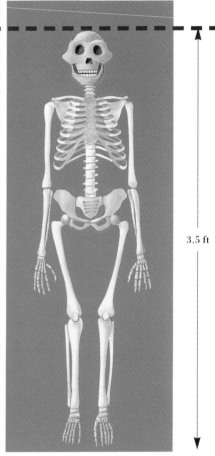

3.5 ft

PYGMY

Long legs, short, basin-shaped pelvis, arms a tad short, broad, well-extended shoulders, barrel-shaped ribcage clearly separated from the pelvis, and a nice head with a big brain.

CHIMPANZEE

Short legs, long feet and hands, pelvis flattened from top to bottom, conical chest cavity set close to the pelvis, narrow shoulders, long arms, somewhat short neck, skull with modest brain, and nice jaws.

GIRL

Short legs, long ribcage, short arms, big head with dainty jaws, large eyes, big brain.

LUCY

Short legs, long feet, short, flaring pelvis, ribcage, shoulders, and neck of a chimpanzee, long arms and big hands, oblique head with modest brain and superb, strong jaws.

HERE'S THE SPARE

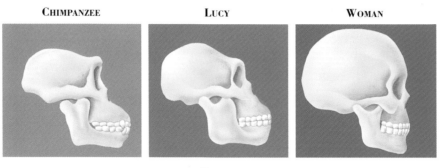

SKULL

Lucy's skull is much like that of a chimpanzee's in terms of size and shape, and its braincase is of about the same size (370 cubic cm.). However, Lucy's face is more robust and longer. Australopithecus afarensis has rather large teeth and solid jaws, indicating that they ate food that was considerably harder than that consumed by chimps. The foramen magnum—the large hole at the base of the skull through which the spinal cord enters the skull and where the base of the skull rests on the first cervical vertebra (atlas)—is located forward in humans but is absent in Lucy. The forward position is a characteristic related to upright walking.

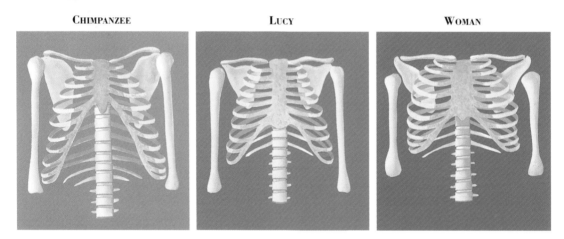

TORSO AND ARMS

Lucy's ribcage is similar to that of a chimp. It is conical in shape and narrows toward the shoulders, which are not extended and wide like those of modern-day women. The bottom of the ribcage is located near the pelvis. The arms are long. The elbow and shoulder joints allow for broad movements of the arms and their various parts. All these characteristics can be related to tree climbing.

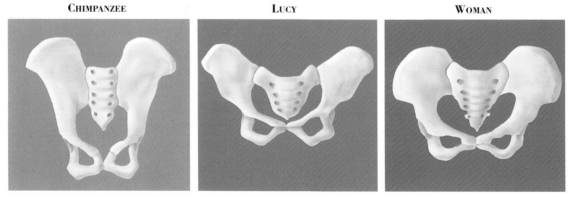

PELVIS

Despite what some people say, Lucy had the pelvis of a human woman; it is without doubt her most "feminine" part. The wings of her pelvis are wider and open upward toward the sides. The sacrum—the group of fused vertebrae that forms the back of the pelvis—is highly developed, for it distributes the weight of the upper part of the body to the pelvis. All these characteristics are related to upright walking.

PARTS DEPARTMENT

Which does Lucy most resemble, the female chimpanzee or the woman? Remember, Lucy is not an intermediary between humans and chimps (and we know chimps are not the direct offspring of australopithecines, nor are they ancestors of humans). Lucy and her species may be related to certain species alive today, but if so they are very ancient parents. But it's hard to avoid the question: is Lucy more like a female ape or a woman? Obviously, she is neither one nor the other. She possesses many characteristics, some that are uniquely her own, some that recall human features, some related to chimps or to species known only from fossil remains. This variety of characteristics indicates a unique species of hominids, one that existed between 4 and 3 million years ago and that was well adapted to its environment.

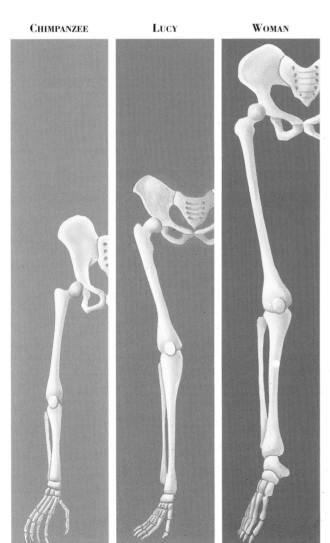

CHIMPANZEE LUCY WOMAN

LEGS
Lucy's femur (thighbone) has a collar, and its shaft—the diaphysis—is slanted. This is the femur of a bipedal creature. However, the knee joint is looser than that of a human woman's. The farther away you move from the hips, the more the bones recall those of a female chimpanzee. Lucy walked on the savanna but was able to climb trees easily.

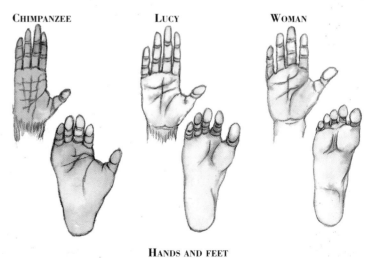

CHIMPANZEE LUCY WOMAN

HANDS AND FEET
Lucy's hands and feet are long, the fingers and toes are extended and curved—all characteristics found in chimps. The shape of the joints responds to the need to securely grab tree branches.

WHAT'S INSIDE YOUR HEAD

Having a big brain is a good thing, but given the choice, having a well-made brain is even better. Like other parts of the body, the brain—the quantity of gray matter—varies a great deal from one individual to another. In fact, the size of the brain is not very useful in evaluating the intelligence of individuals of the same species. On the other hand, the average brain size is a useful piece of information when comparing different species. Brain size can have great significance in terms of intelligence, adaptation, and evolution.

IS NOT ALWAYS BETTER

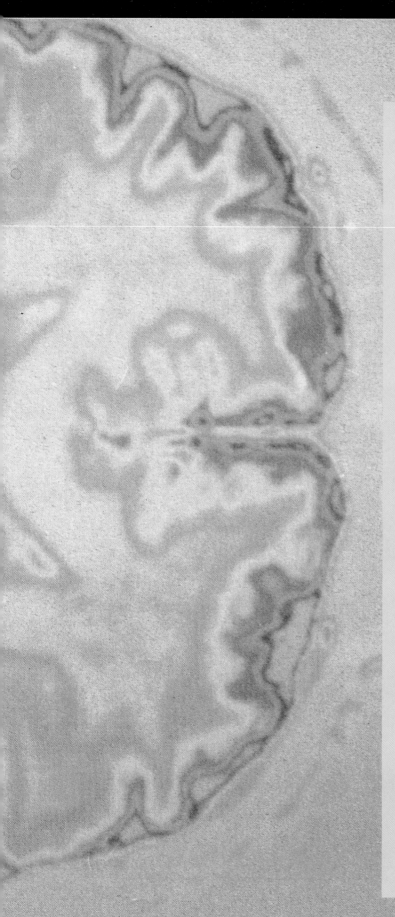

Coping with others takes a lot of brains

Why do apes have big brains? Because they live in groups. Living in groups implies complicated relationships. It means having to constantly adapt to the wishes, intentions, and moods of others. In a general sense, having an intense social life and making intelligent use of the environment requires a well-developed brain. It's also directly related to having a rich and diversified diet.

Lucy: a little brain full of activity

The size of the brain of *Australopithecus afarensis*, estimated on the basis of the braincase, varies between 360 and 440 cubic centimeters. This is about the same as that of a chimp, at most only a little better. However, examination of the marks left by the brain sections on the skull walls of *A. afarensis* indicates that there were important differences with respect to chimps. The asymmetries (unbalanced proportions) between the right and left side are more striking; the parietal side—the side that processes and integrates information from the sensory areas (hearing and sight)—is more extensive. These characteristics indicate a well-made brain with a potential intelligence capacity that, from the human point of view, is evolved. Given what we know about what chimps can do in their social strategies, their mastery of the environment, or their use of tools it's easy to imagine that *A. afarensis* performed just as well. It's fair to say that Lucy was rather smart!

Why are we always so interested in the sex life of others?
It does seem that Lucy and her kind weren't always monogamous.
And she certainly never wore a wedding veil (never mind the dress).
Let's look at what may have been going on a few million years ago.

LUCY AND LOUIS SITTING IN A TREE . . .

WAS LOUIS BIGGER THAN LUCY?

In monogamous primate species—those in which males and females form lifetime couples, such as the gibbons and humans—males and females are about the same size and have "normal" canine teeth. In primate species that are not monogamous, things are different. The females are smaller than the males, and the males have large canine teeth—they use them to fight (including battles over females). Gorillas are a fine example: the males form harems. No surprise, then, that the males grow to twice the size of the females and have far larger canines. Chimpanzees go halfway: the males tolerate one another, and there is some sexual promiscuity, so the males are a little bigger than the females, and their canines are a little bigger, too. These differences are less pronounced in the case of pygmy chimps, whose sexual manners are less aggressive.

DID LUCY HAVE ONE BOYFRIEND OR MANY?

Lucy and Louis were closer to chimps and gorillas in terms of height differences (he was bigger), but in terms of their canines they were closer to the pygmy chimps. The similar size of their canines suggests monogamy; the difference in their sizes suggests that things were otherwise. It seems likely that Lucy did not have a single Louis—she wasn't necessarily monogamous. As in other matters, it's too bad she didn't leave us a diary.

PALEOMATRIMONIAL ANNOUNCEMENTS

The differences in size between the sexes bears the fancy name of sexual dimorphism. Despite its highfalutin moniker, the subject has more than a little to do with reproduction. It's an area of great interest to paleoanthropologists.

Lucy and her girlfriends stood between 3 feet 4 inches and 4 feet tall and weighed somewhere between 55 and 80 pounds. Their boyfriends, on the other hand, were between 4 feet and 4 feet 8 inches tall and tipped the scales, so to speak, at around 65 to 100 pounds. Of course, these approximate figures do not take into account the important variations possible in single members of the species.

I adore tall men like my Louis!

According to certain American paleoanthropologists, Lucy walked and ran and lived with a single male. These scientists believe that her sexuality was basically that of a contemporary human and that she had all the attributes usually considered necessary to attract a mate: breasts, hips, and buttocks. Lucy had all the features of a small woman. But according to other American scientists and also to certain French scientists, Lucy didn't have a bipedal position similar to that of human women. So she did not have an upright posture and walked by swaying her hips.

THE BIRDS, THE BEES, AND ALSO THE CHIMPS

When a female chimp enters her period of ovulation, known as estrus, and becomes fertile, her genitals swell and take on a vivid color. Because of the semi-upright position of the chimp's body, this fertility message is clearly visible to males. The posture and mode of locomotion of the pygmy chimp are comparable to those of the chimps, but their sexual manners are somewhat human. They reproduce in all positions, especially face to face. This activity is possible because the genitals of the pygmy chimp face the front of the pelvis, and not the rear, as is the case in all other apes. To compensate for this, the penis of the males can easily adjust direction following whatever position may be taken during copulation. Pygmy chimps demonstrate a lively interest in love games: females have prolonged periods of sexual receptivity, periods that extend beyond the time of estrus. These are characteristics also found among humans.

LUCY AND LOUIS AND THESE "FACTS" OF LIFE

Lucy and Louis are not the kind to kiss and tell: their stories are completely private. Love preserves its mystery. All this by way of admitting that scientists aren't too sure.

Based on the sexual dimorphism of their species—Lucy was smaller than Louis—scientists think that Lucy and Louis had a sex life more or less similar to that of pygmy chimps and humans, two species that have very similar sexual habits. Beyond that, we can only guess. Scientists have determined that Lucy was about 20 years old when she died. Were she and Louis parents? Was she holding out, waiting for someone a little more her height?

NATURE'S LAW: TO EACH HER (OR HIS) OWN

You'd never catch me doing anything like that!

HEEEERE'S LUCY

A HOMINID PRESS CONFERENCE

A HAIRLESS FACE SHOWS MORE EMOTION

Apes are very noisy animals that communicate a great deal, and they are helped in doing so by a developed brain. Like humans, they have relatively hairless faces. They use various facial expressions to display their emotions and intentions, and they use their bodies to assume postures, some filled with significance. They touch one another a great deal, with plenty of hand touching, embraces, and even kisses, especially among chimps. Their relationships rely on a clever mixture of aggression and reconciliation. In some species, including the pygmy chimps, individuals intervene to help end conflicts, like genuine peacemakers. Chimps show great skill at forming alliances and also at staging sneaky plots; they manage to lie—meaning to communicate false information—when doing so serves their interests. The only thing they lack is language.

IT'S NOT NECESSARY TO SPEAK TO COMMUNICATE

With humans, the process of communication is channeled through language. Indeed, we are so specialized at language that we have difficulties "understanding" the methods of communication used by chimps and other apes, methods composed of gestures, attitudes, glances, and—thanks again to their hairless faces—facial expressions, the meanings of which are lost on us. We do know that apes also use vocal messages to convey various information. However, according to our present understanding of apes' communication, such messages cannot be compared to language, which is a type of exchange based on the use of grammar and vocal symbols. We do not know the methods of communication used by Lucy and her friends. It seems likely that their ability to communicate was at least as sophisticated as that of chimps. Lucy lived in a relatively open environment, the savanna, where individuals must spread out over large areas in search of food and where a good knowledge of the surroundings is a prime necessity. But that life also requires an elaborate system of communication to maintain social structure. The makeup of the brain of *Australopithecus afarensis* seems to indicate an increased capability for understanding the personality and intentions of other individuals. Beyond this, little more can be said: the fossils remain hopelessly mute. In the end, we may never know who spoke the first word. Did Lucy speak? Probably not, but she was certainly able to communicate.

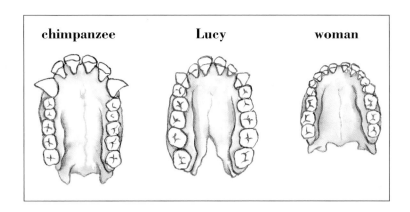

chimpanzee   Lucy   woman

THE TALE OF THE TEETH

The tale of life can be told through teeth. You might be surprised by how much teeth really have to say. Let's begin with size. The incisors of *Australopithecus afarensis* are a little bit smaller than those of chimps. Chimps eat a lot of fruit and need good incisors to cut into it. *A. afarensis* did not necessarily eat less fruit (though that seems likely), but probably showed a preference for smaller-size fruit.

The molars of *A. afarensis* were larger than those of chimps. They have rounded ridges, are covered with a thick layer of enamel, and are held in place by strong roots. All these characteristics indicate that Lucy chewed her food vigorously, which makes plenty of sense since the plants on the savanna are rather hard. Such energetic chewing also explains the strong jaws and well-built face of Lucy's species.

THE ENAMEL REVEALS IT SECRETS

Food leaves visible traces on the surface of dental enamel. Examined under a microscope, the teeth of *A. afarensis* reveal striations and tiny pits as well as smooth sections. Comparison of these traces with those that can be seen on the teeth of chimps and baboons indicates that Lucy probably ate fruit, leaves, and "underground foods," meaning tubers (plants like potatoes), onions, roots, and bulbs of plants that were abundant on the tree-bearing savannas of Africa.

HOW OLD IS LUCY WHEN THE TOOTH FAIRY COMES?

Let's look at a section of the crown of one of Lucy's molars. A good microscope shows us ridges and regular bands that apparently correspond to the growth of the individual—almost like the rings of a tree. According to these marks *A. afarensis* had periods of life comparable to those of chimps. Study of the sequence of development of milk teeth and permanent teeth confirms the observations made based on the structure of the enamel. Moreover, we know that weaning occurs when the first molar appears and that by then the brain has nearly finished its physical development. In the case of Lucy and her "family," this took place sometime between 4 and 5 years of age, instead of 6 to 7 years, as is normal for children today. Real gossips, these teeth! They can also report a lot of things concerning the health of an individual—dietary deficiencies, certain illnesses, and other important life events—as well as certain facts, such as the sex of the individual. As we said, these teeth are really talking.

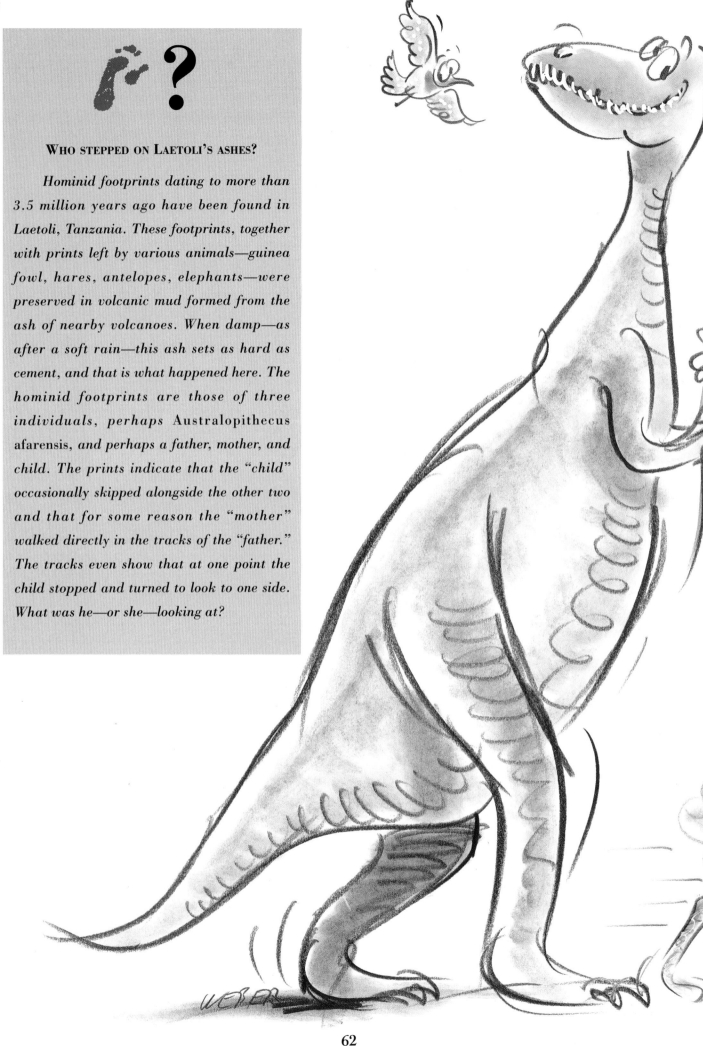

WHO STEPPED ON LAETOLI'S ASHES?

Hominid footprints dating to more than 3.5 million years ago have been found in Laetoli, Tanzania. These footprints, together with prints left by various animals—guinea fowl, hares, antelopes, elephants—were preserved in volcanic mud formed from the ash of nearby volcanoes. When damp—as after a soft rain—this ash sets as hard as cement, and that is what happened here. The hominid footprints are those of three individuals, perhaps Australopithecus afarensis, and perhaps a father, mother, and child. The prints indicate that the "child" occasionally skipped alongside the other two and that for some reason the "mother" walked directly in the tracks of the "father." The tracks even show that at one point the child stopped and turned to look to one side. What was he—or she—looking at?

WALK THAT WALK

Standing upright on your hind legs is one thing: walking and running that way is something else again. That's why scientists emphasize the difference between posture—the way you stand—and locomotion—the way you move. Many animals are able to stand upright and do so to get a better view of their surroundings, to threaten enemies, or to reach food. Animals can also be trained to do this, as shown by various kinds of circus animals. Actually being bipedal is something else and requires special anatomic adaptations.

IT'S SAFER TO MOVE BENEATH THE BRANCH THAN ON IT

Among bipeds, only humans move with their trunk in a truly vertical position. This is an ancient posture, and it comes down to us from life in the trees. By 15 million years ago our ancestors had reached a large size. This size posed various problems when moving along tree branches, and it became safer to hang from them. This is the reason why hominoids (gibbons, gorillas, chimps, orangutans, and humans) have lost their tail. It also explains why their ribcage is narrow from front to back but wide from side to side, why their shoulder blades are shifted to the back, and why their spinal column contains few lumbar vertebrae. The vertical position has an old family history.

THE ORIGINS OF BIPEDALISM

All hominoids can walk in the bipedal position, at least occasionally, when on the ground or when moving across thick tree branches. This was probably true for the common ancestor of hominoids. Bipedalism probably stems from our life in trees. But it was with the australopithecines that it developed and extended from the forest to the savanna. And it was early humans who perfected it. Like all hominids, Lucy had a bipedal position. And it worked out fine for her.

If you ask me, I walk better than some of these bipeds.

Lucy's bipedal posture

As we know, Lucy walks with both feet planted firmly on the ground. She stands erect on her small legs and moves with a swaying gait. Her hips and shoulders swivel with each stride. All her movements reveal a continuous attempt to balance various parts of her body. There's a whole lot of shaking going on when Lucy walks. Traveling like this required the expenditure of a great deal of energy, and long walks were thus out of the question.

Forget about running fast with this type of anatomy. But once at the bottom of a tree, Lucy's anatomy reveals its advantages. She is able to climb easily and hang on comfortably. She is really the hominid queen in terms of acrobatics. To conclude, it's obvious that one could hardly imagine better biomechanics for traveling across the savanna.

"EVE'S" BIPEDAL POSTURE

Tall and slender, Eve walks taking big strides with her long legs, which she hardly bends. The movement of her body speaks with eloquence of grace and harmony. Her hips and shoulders maintain superb stability, which favors long walks. This efficient anatomy is suited for extended journeys by combining economy of energy with endurance. The fine engineering also provides an incredible running machine for bursts of speed. The alternate movements of the arm and leg from opposite sides assure a fast gait. The erect body, chest facing forward, relative lack of hair, and ability to perspire abundantly favor the efficient elimination of the body heat produced during running. Eve is a high-performance athlete on flat ground, which compensates for her poor skill at climbing trees. Well, you can't have everything.

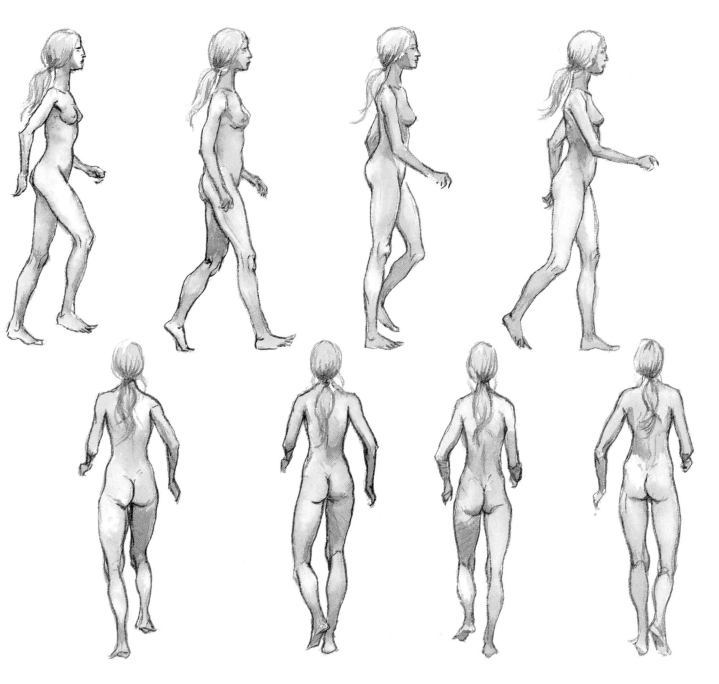

EVOLUTION DOESN'T DELIVER PERFECTION

Lucy had a very wide pelvis. Does this mean she could give birth easily? The fact that she had a large pelvis and that the newborn had a small head would certainly suggest that everything was well-coordinated for an easy delivery. Unfortunately for Lucy, there may have been complications because of her bipedal posture.

A SACRUM GUARANTEED TO TURN A BABY'S HEAD

Walking is a matter of mechanics, more precisely biomechanics. In the case of upright bipeds like hominids, the mass of various parts of the body is piled up along the spinal column. This is why the vertebrae become bigger and bigger as they go down from the cervical region to the pelvis. The vertebrae fuse at the level of the pelvis to form the sacrum. The sacrum is large and markedly recessed (located to the rear). It serves to transmit the weight of the upper part of the body to the femur through the wings of the pelvis. The shorter the distance between the sacrum and the femur, the better the mechanics of walking. All this makes walking upright easier, but it does nothing to ease the delivery of babies.

In bipeds, the sacrum occupies a somewhat more frontal position and forms a promontory that invades the space needed for the passage of the newborn, which is called the little pelvis. This passage is shaped like a big kidney bean. Here lie the difficulties for

the unborn baby. The head must rotate in order to align itself with the greatest diagonal width of the little pelvis. This complex contortion is dangerous, and during birth the mother suffers tremendously. Some paleoanthropologists think that Lucy delivered without difficulty. Others do not. In any case, nature does not always seem kind to women, and such may have been the case with Lucy, too.

DR. LEUTENEGGER
This delivery will be a snap. The brain of the baby—and, hey, it's a boy—doesn't weigh more than 120 grams (but don't ask how I know that). Even though his skull is a tad larger than that of a baby chimp, the mother's pelvis is wide enough.

DR. TAGUE
The head of the newborn must be inclined, and in some cases it has to take quite an angle. That is unusual, but it works well enough for the little acrobat.

MATERNITY WARD

DRS. SCHMID AND HÄUSLER
Despite the fact that we're in this photo, we don't believe that Lucy could deliver because in our opinion Lucy is a male. The author of this book doesn't agree, and nor does anyone else. The real question is why am I wearing two watches but no gloves?

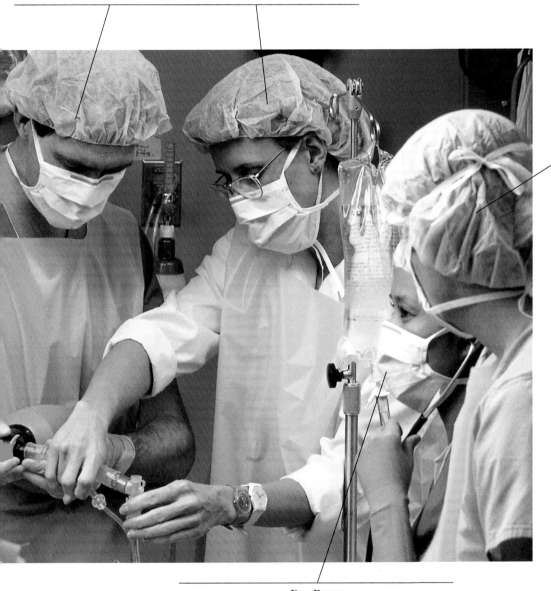

DR. LOVEJOY
Cool! There's nothing to fear with those hippy hips and the minimal noggin on that newborn. We're going to need some wiggling action down the road, so to speak, but I see no problems in the immediate future of our newest family member.

DR. BERGE
Despite that sacrum, all of this will be okay. You know, because of the position and shape of the sacrum, the baby won't go toward the back of the pelvis but forward, just like with modern females. Sometimes I really wonder about that sacrum: a few design changes and generations of women would feel a lot less pain.

Any resemblance to existing Homo sapiens *is purely accidental.*

ONE CHILD MAY BE MORE DIFFICULT THAN MANY

In mammals, reproduction is characterized by one of two basic tendencies: some mammal species give birth to many babies and quickly leave them alone in nature; others have a single offspring that they care for over a long period of time. Naturalists have come up with complex equations and some confusing coefficients to better describe these tendencies. The coefficient "r" is applied to prolific species, while the coefficient "K" is used for those who make so much fuss about their little ones. Apes are the "K"-type mammals par excellence. A female ape delivers a single baby at the end of its period of pregnancy. The newborns are rather precocious, but this doesn't prevent them for suckling for several years. After weaning, a long childhood begins, also spent alongside the mother. All the periods of life are relatively long: gestation, weaning, childhood, sexual maturity, teens, adulthood, and old age.

This sort of lifestyle, with its long childhood, which is much like an apprenticeship, often goes hand-in-hand with large-brained mammals. By contrast, "r"-type species are most often small in size, live a short and highly active life, reproduce rapidly, and bring into the world numerous offspring. The size of their populations varies strongly according to the resources in the environment. Rodents,

r

MOUSE
Hundreds of little ones each year.

RABBIT
About fifty little ones each year.

CAT
About twenty little ones each year.

PIG
A dozen little ones each year.

WOLF
Five or six little ones each year.

Z

IS FOR KIDS

rabbits, and their predators are typical "r"-type animals. While both may be mammals, there is a good distance between man and mouse. The epitome of the "K" strategy consists in involving the fathers in the education of the young ones. This does not always work out, but there are shining examples.

THE "K" LUCY

Perhaps the most "K" of the apes are humans. It takes nearly twenty years to make an adult human; with apes, it takes about fifteen years to raise a little one. In all cases, the education, social life, and brain size are remarkably developed. Lucy and her little ones had a life similar to that of the big apes. Therefore, it is probable that she took good care of her children. The pregnancy lasted between thirty-five and forty weeks; childhood lasted until 4 years of age; sexual maturity arrived at around age 11, with the first born around 14; life expectancy—assuming no unpleasant accidents—was around 30 years.

The *Australopithecus afarensis* were very "K," and the life of a "Little Lucy" must have been terrific.

→**K**

LEOPARD
o to three little ones each year.

DEER
One each year.

HORSE
One every two years.

GORILLA
One every four to five years.

WOMAN
*One baby every five to six years.**

* Before the advances of modern medicine

LUCY, LUKE, LOUIS, LOUISE . . .

How can we reconstruct the social life of *Australopithecus afarensis*? It's a little tricky because a variety of lifestyles can be found among the hominoids: orangutans are rather solitary; chimps, bonobo chimps, and humans form communities; gorillas prefer harems; while gibbons cherish living in couples.

WHAT SIZE IS RIGHT?

We can easily say what the *A. afarensis* are not: they are not solitary. Indeed, no species in Africa is, particularly among those living in more or less open environments. Life as a monogamous couple, with Mr. and Mrs. *A. afarensis* living alone on their own small territory, also seems unlikely; that would indicate that they were of about the same size. Furthermore, there are no indications on the woodland savannas of the existence of small love-nests. Life in a harem, with a big dominant male, would imply males twice as large as the females, which is not the case with *A. afarensis*. What remains is life in groups composed of several adult males and females. This is the type of social organization most frequently found among apes living on woodland savannas (such as baboons and vervets), among chimpanzees, and among humans. Group life offers many important advantages with respect to dealing with predators and rivals for food in a fairly difficult environment.

STAND BY YOUR CLAN

The fact that *A. afarensis* males possess less prominent canines confirms the existence of groups composed of several males connected by family ties. In this type of group males tolerate one another and control sexual competition. This is observed in the case of chimps, bonobos, and humans, too. Members remain in their family group their entire life. It must have been similar in the *A. afarensis* groups. Sometimes the females leave their family to join another group. During a pleasant spring 3 million years ago, Lucy may have left her family to look for a fiancé.

RELATIONS WITH THE IN-LAWS

Did Lucy make friends with the Louises and LuAnns of her world, or did she relate only to the members of her family? Nobody knows, but the nature of the social structure and the existence of competition offer several clues.

When competition is intense, females who are not related by family ties tend to avoid one another, as among chimps. When the resources can be defended by many, the females tend to support one another, as among the bonobos. In situations where the resources are equally spread, as is the case among humans, one can conceive male-female relations reinforced in a kind of irregular monogamy within a group containing several couples. What we know about the social system of *A. afarensis* suggests a life similar to that observed in chimps and bonobos; namely, a community in which the individuals form temporary associations according to the circumstances of the moment, meaning they form small groups of two up to several individuals. For further details we would have to read Lucy's diary!

NAP TIME

It's too hot in the afternoon for any activity. Better take a nice nap in a leafy tree and let the torrid hours pass while digesting quietly. Preparations for the night are more serious, involving the making of leafy nests to protect against the cold.

MEALS

To have a bite to eat, A. afarensis use their developed jaws. They also know how to use primitive tools. Depending on the food they find and its abundance, they eat in a little circle or in a larger group. Things can get quite cozy, especially when huddled around some prey or a termite nest. Such groups are also a good time to meet possible mates.

THE BATH

Only those who are dirty take a bath. Chimps hate water, while bonobos like it. As for humans, well, it's variable. A. afarensis visited the borders of bodies of water (as we'll see, such places were not always the safest).

CLEANING UP

Apes do not like being dirty. They use leaves as toilet paper. They also use leaves to clean dirt from various parts of their body.

THE LIFE

DEFENSE

Even in the tops of trees, security can't be guaranteed. Panthers and leopards are fond of hominids (and not in a good way). However, hominids aren't easy to catch, especially when they're in a group. An isolated individual takes some risks, particularly a female or child. But as soon as there are two or more males, the tide turns against any hungry predator, no matter how long its teeth.

DELOUSING

Delousing is a big issue for Lucy and her friends. It helps to get rid of parasites. It also serves to intensify the bonds between males and females as well as strengthening the group by providing care for everyone.

NURSING

As adults, females become full-time mothers. When not pregnant, they're usually nursing a little one. Weaning takes place at the age of 4 or 5 years, which liberates the mother from suckling but announces another impending pregnancy. Luckily, there's only one baby at a time!

RAVELING

ources of food grow
arce during the dry season,
d the search for food requires
nger excursions across the savanna.
he bipedal position helps in these trips.
uring such periods, A. afarensis communities
robably divided into smaller groups, increasing
e chance of finding food but also increasing
e chance of danger. Fortunately, predators
e less active during daylight hours!

73

FORMAL DINNER

Find a dead, small antelope.

•

Climb a fruit tree
(without ladder, for greater authenticity)
and gather some fruit.

•

While up the tree,
take advantage of your position to
grab any magpie or cuckoo eggs.

•

For dessert, we recommend antelope brains
served on a bed of crisp leaves.

MMM-MMM GOOD

SUNDAY BRUNCH

Scratch around in the dirt—
use your nails if they're long enough,
but a sturdy stick will be even better
and more realistic.

•

Grasp the larva of an insect
between two fingers.

•

Squeeze as needed and eat.

•

Continue scratching,
keeping an eye out for tasty tubers.

•

You can end the meal with juicy berries.
*(Ask around first to see if anyone remembers
which are poisonous.)*

SNACK TIME

Place yourself directly beneath a walnut tree.

•

Look down: find fallen nuts.

•

Select a suitable rock and smash them
(watch your fingers).

•

Recommended side dishes include tender roots,
bulbs, tubers, and eggs
(without the shell, but don't use the rock).

•

*Note: All of this will go down
more easily following ample chewing.*

DINING OUT WITH LUCY

SAVANNA PARTY TIME

Collect a good number of termites
on a long stick.

•

Swallow them as fast as you can
to avoid getting stung.

•

Served with tender leaves,
this makes a delicious seasonal meal.
*If lucky, you can add a small bird
freshly fallen from its nest;
any juicy fruits or figs are guaranteed
to delight your guests.*

FRIEND OR FOE?

OCCASIONALLY EVERYBODY HELPS HER- (HIM)SELF TO NATURE'S BUFFET

Baboons, chimpanzees, and humans lived in East Africa eating fruit, leaves, tubers, insects, and meat. All of them were interested in at least some of this food. Therefore, they were competitors. This competition didn't necessarily mean that individuals fought one another, but blows were not unheard of.

WHAT HAPPENS WHEN THE BUFFET IS BARE?

When mother nature is generous, the competition is not too fierce. But in times of shortage, when seasonal changes or climatic disturbances have made certain foods scarce, food resources that don't usually represent an important part of the diet become vital. The ability of humans to hunt effectively, of chimps to eat more leaves, and of baboons to crunch up more tubers and roots have proved vital during critical moments of their evolution.

In Lucy's time there were few, if any, baboons and no chimps. Lucy ate a variety of foods, preferring the hard food of the savanna. This proved to be an advantage with respect to the competitor apes of her time (geladas, baboons, colobines) as well as other contemporary hominids we're still discovering. You must also take into account the wart hogs and other fans of fruits and roots. As long as there was abundance, no problem. But when food begins to be scarce and the freeloaders arrive, well, then . . .

Lucy's garden was
abundant and varied.
There were creepers
with tubers, palms,
almonds, bulbs, onions,
herbaceous plants, pulpy
fruits, wild grasses,
and of course all kinds
of nutritious trees.

In Lewis Carroll's *Through the Looking Glass*, the Red Queen tells Alice, "You see, it takes all the running you can do, to keep in the same place."

RUNNING IN PLACE
ON THE EVOLUTIONARY
TREADMILL

Even if we were to travel back in time and visit Lucy on her savanna, it would be difficult to understand the drama that unfolded there. Lucy lived in an environment teeming with a great diversity of creatures. These ecological communities evolved as well, and it's here where we can call upon the model of the Red Queen.

RUNNING IN PLACE TO HOLD YOUR PLACE

Lucy and her companions ate all kinds of things, with a preference for hard food; some of the hominids more or less closely related to *Australopithecus afarensis* showed a greater tendency to eat other types of food. Around 3 to 2.5 million years ago, early humans and the first robust australopithecines appeared. Early humans were able to take from the provisions of *A. afarensis* while at the same time hunting for meat. For their part, the robust australopithecines drew upon the food resources of *A. afarensis*, too, but they were able to eat really hard food that was less accessible to other hominids. As long as there was abundance, all went well, but . . .

LUCY LEAVES THE FIELD

The competition became tough when the climate deteriorated around 3 million years ago. *A. afarensis* was not inclined to eat meat, nor could it chew very hard food, so it became disadvantaged and began to disappear. For nearly 1 million years *A. afarensis* was able to "run" fast enough to preserve its ecological niche. Nevertheless when competition becomes intense in an ecological community species that have certain specializations end up overtaking others. However, these species will in turn be overtaken when climatic changes make them pay for their specialization, and so there will be again a time favoring the more generalized species. The Red Queen's race never ends, but Lucy's time runs out.

A ROYAL TREADMILL

Much of evolution has to do with competition among species. When different species compete for the same food resources, each seeks to evolve strategies to get its share of the food while also avoiding predators. In a stable situation, with enough food for all, competing species become involved in a kind of "treadmill," each doing its best to adapt to the changes in its competitors. Biologists call this treadmill of competition the Red Queen hypothesis; of course, anything that changes the situation will change the terms of the competition and probably favor one of the species and not all.

It seems that the art director of this book can't get it through her head that my name is Lucy, not Alice.

79

Secret File
LUCY
Australopithecus afarensis
OFFICIAL DEATH INQUIRY

HOW DID LUCY DIE?

**REPORT ON THE DEATH OF LUCY
AND A FAMILY OF
AUSTRALOPITHECUS AFARENSIS**

Statement of Maurice Taïeb, geologist

"We've already been through all this. One fine day in the fall of 1975 I was on Locality 333 of Hadar. It was there that I saw all the fossils. It was hard to believe. I bent down to seek clues. First, I picked up the remains of at least a dozen individuals. There were adult males and females as well as children. An *Australopithecus afarensis* 'family,' which proved that they lived in a community. But due to some misfortune they had been washed away by the floodtide. Everything seemed to indicate that they liked the coolness of the vegetation along the river bank. But a sudden rise of the water, perhaps due to a tropical storm, killed all of them. The study of the sediment and the state of the bones shows that they were carried along by tumultuous waves. It was a family outing that had a tragic end.

As for Lucy, I have no idea. She didn't belong to this family. She died in a different place, Locality 288. Her bones were arranged along a little channel. I honestly don't know how she died. The ground has yielded her bones, and the natural elements have done the rest. This poor little australopithecine died very young, in her twentieth spring.

Believe me, I had nothing to do with these deaths. I have a good alibi: I was born 3 million years later. In fact, you should thank me for having helped discover these traces of the past."

TECHNICAL DATA

Name: *Australopithecus afarensis*

Nickname: *Lucy*

Date of birth: *3.2 million years ago*

Date of death: *3.2 million years ago*

Place of birth: *Afar, Ethiopia*

Place of death: *Afar, Ethiopia*

Sex: *female*

Weight: *60 pounds*

Height: *3.5 feet*

Distinguishing marks: *hairy*

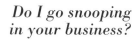

Do I go snooping in your business?

I, Lucy, being of sound mind and little bo
would like to make some revelations and
recommendations to future species.

First, my name was not Lucy and even
less AL 288-1.

I'm sorry to bequeath to future women a
difficult delivery, especially to you humans who
have such large heads.

I bequeath my jaws and my beautiful
teeth to the robust australopithecines. Humans
will neglect proper chewing and will end up at
the dentist.

Lucy Australopithecus afarensis. Afar. Ethiopie

Lucy Australopi... ...arensis. Afar. Eth...

...us afarensis. ...

Lucy Austral...

...opie

BEFORE THE GRAVE

I knew an Africa that vibrated with great ecological riches. Hopefully humans will notice these wonders and know how to use their big brains to preserve them.

I'm getting sleepy, and everything around me seems to be growing blurry. Well, my time has come. I can just make out in the distance some bipeds moving across the savanna. I can barely see them: they move slowly, but they certainly seem sure of themselves. Nice gait, too.

I'm passing on at the dawn of humanity . . .

Yours forever,

Lucy

Lucy *Australopithecus afarensis. Afar. Ethiopie*

Lucy *Australopithecus afarensis. Afar. Ethi*

OH, THE PLACES YOU'LL GO

Lucy's species vanished as early humans emerged. Was she their ancestor? Paleoanthropologists don't agree on her position as grandmother or great-aunt. Such a small and charming hominid would make an adorable (anthropological) grandmother. But, alas, research is not based on sentiments. Scientists have divided up the *Australopithecus afarensis*, placing them on this or that branch of the hominid family, locating their fossils in different lineages . . . like heirs quarreling over the terms of a will. And which is the ancestor of Lucy herself, *A. anamensis* or *Ardipithecus ramidus*? Nobody really knows. It seems that Lucy and her relatives were living among the descendants of the robust australopithecines, which disappeared perhaps around 1 million years ago following a period of fatally cold weather. Early humans survived because of their terrific physical and mental powers. They are the only apes able to live in all climates and all environments. With their big legs, skillful hands, and cultures, they become superpredators and install themselves at the top of any ecological system. Africa quickly becomes too small for them: as early as 2 million years ago, humans had already made their way across the entire ancient Eurasian world. Only 500,000 years elapse between the man of Lake Rudolf (now Lake Turkana) in Kenya and the most ancient Java men. Moving little by little, let's say one mile per generation, humanity advances nonstop from its African cradle to the Far East and eventually through the rest of the world.

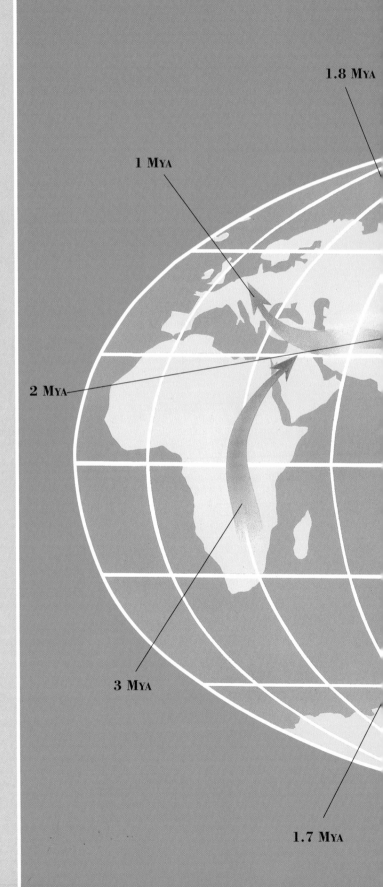

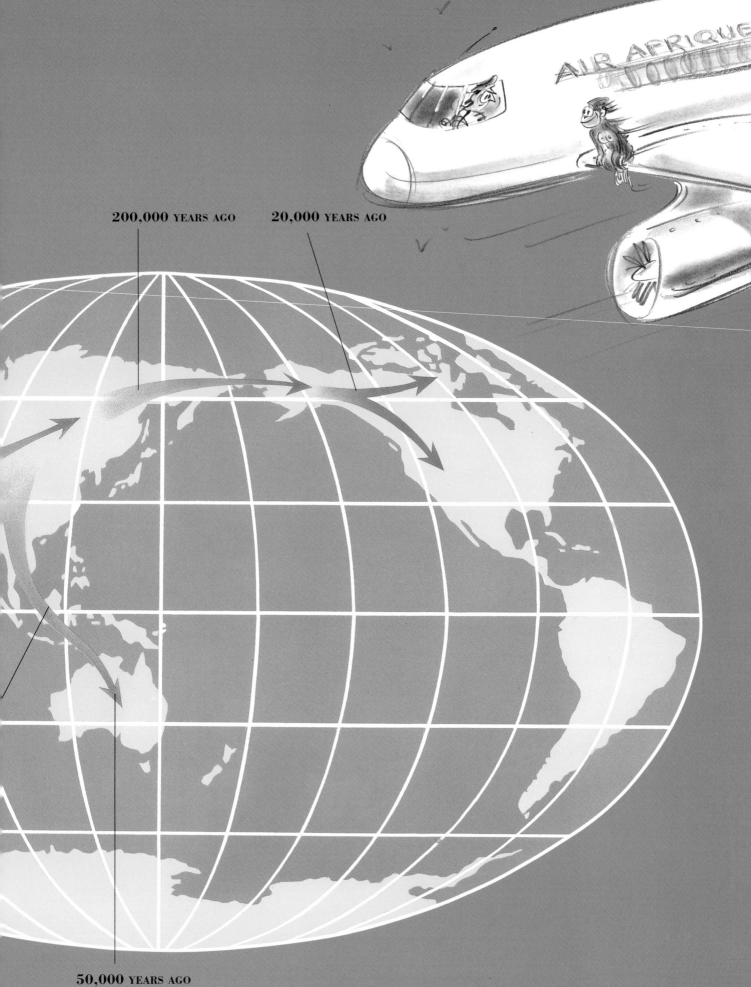

The history of the hominids is a megaproduction that is like a crime movie. Most of the performers get killed off, one by one, but by different murder weapons: some are done in by competition from other species, some meet their doom as a result of changes in climate. For example, all of the actors who clung to their

roles on the branches of trees were eliminated when the trees were swept off the stage.

As for humans, they prove adaptable to any role in any drama and spread over the vast earthly stage using their magnificent legs and powers of locomotion. But unfortunately, as superstars, they took on a very nasty attitude, despising the extras

and the stagesets. If the day ever comes when they're the only ones left in the production, it might be too late to shout, Cut!

ORANGUTANS
"I may be big and lazy, but I made a movie with Clint Eastwood. Not bad for a debut! Clearly, fighting is not my thing. And considering the trends of the current human film industry, there aren't too many opportunities for me to make my day."

CHIMPANZEES
"I'm a serious creature and a real star (although I've thought about changing agents). That was me alongside Tarzan every time; and as Bonzo I helped give Ronald Reagan his big chance. As for a superstar role I still have to wait a millennium or so to appear in the actual Planet of the Apes, but next time it's going to be for real."

GORILLAS
"Sweet as I am—just ask anyone—I've been typecast for years as a villain, big and mean. Sure, King Kong is a great movie, but in terms of reality it's baloney. I won't say anything about plans for a rematch with Godzilla. So I'm a big hairy ape. Big deal. I'm probably nicer than a lot of the people you run into in the mall. You call me a monster?"

EXIT THE WORLD'S STAGE
WHO'S STILL HERE)

BONOBOS
"I'm the latest discovery, and while I may be small I'm packed with star quality. Even so, my agent says I shouldn't quit my day job too soon— says my morals are too high for any of those Hollywood productions. It's a jungle out there."

GIBBONS
"Where do we come from and where are we going? Such are the deep questions we ask ourselves. We have this kind of identity problem. Among hominoids, we're the ones who never appear on movie posters. We're only extras, and half the time they leave us hanging around on the set."

WOMEN
"All of a sudden I feel a little lonely. There's no intermission in this movie, and all these apes are getting a bit testy. They don't seem satisfied with the roles we've given them, and some of them blame us for the damage that's been done to the stage set. Maybe they're right. Well, I guess we're all in the middle of a big drama, and no one knows how it's going to end."

BABOONS
"We're never cast as good guys, always as brutes and evil characters. It's true that we're quite impressive with our prominent canines. But we're certainly not the Dracula of the savannas. What's so bad about being a big baboon? Anyway, when actors in minor roles are made the stars, you can bet the reviews will be bad."

For historical cast changes, see pages 12-13

THE END ?

Cultural evolution begins with the early humans around 2.5 million years ago. Its pace was slow at first, but the process was destined to continuously accelerate. About 1 million years were needed to pass

GLASS

MONEY

HOUSING

STEAM

PRINTING

A

THE COMPASS

W N E S

THE CAR

THE AIRPLANE

ELECTRICITY

MOVIES

MEDICINE

TV

COMPUTERS

SPACE TRAVEL

from the first tools to the use of fire; but fewer than 100 years went by between the introduction of electricity and the harnessing of the atom.

AND TOMORROW?

Can evolution be predicted? In these pages we've taken a look at human evolution. And it's clear that we humans truly have evolved. Did our evolution—meaning the path traveled since Lucy—follow some carefully drafted plan, or was it the result of unpredictable accidents? If we can use science to determine what caused human evolution in the past, why not look the other way, toward the future, following a scenario that would extend the evolutionary process?

In which direction should we seek our future? Perhaps it's in the stars or just the atmosphere of this planet—our continued survival depends on the health of our sun and the quality of the air we breath. As in the past, the weather of the future may determine not just how we dress but what we look like. And if future generations travel through space and even live on other planets, what effect will that have on their bodies? Or is our future evolution inside our own bodies, in our genes? As we learn more about preventing and even predicting disease we may find ways to make the human body healthier. And even if nothing else changes, some scientists claim we're becoming less hairy. In a few million years both men and women may be completely hairless, bald on top and all over. That might not be so bad—one fewer thing to worry about each morning. But no matter how we change, Lucy would still recognize us, just as we recognize her: standing upright on the surface of our planet.

My poor Louis, what have they done to you?

Was Lucy religious? Because she didn't talk, much less write, we can be sure she had no "religion." But since the dawn of time humans have created myths to explain their existence. All peoples, even those living in the most isolated areas of our planet, have created stories of the creation of the universe and of humans. Such stories are called cosmogonies, and all cosmogonies are part of the larger systems of beliefs that are the world's religions.

CREATION ACCORDING TO THE OLD TESTAMENT

"In the beginning God created the heaven and the earth. And the earth was without form, and void; and darkness was upon the face of the deep. And the Spirit of God moved upon the face of the waters. . . . And God said, Let us make man in our image, after our likeness: and let them have dominion over the fish of the sea, and over the fowl of the air, and over the cattle, and over all the earth, and over every creeping thing that creepth upon the earth. . . . And the Lord God said, It is not good that the man should be alone; I will make him an help meet for him. . . . And the Lord God . . . made he a woman, and brought her unto the man."
Bible, authorized King James version

CREATION ACCORDING TO THE KORAN

"He who has made everything which he has created most good: He began the creation of man with nothing more than clay."
Koran, surah XXXII
OR
"And God has created every animal from water. Of them there are some that creep on their bellies; some that walk on two legs; and some that walk on four."
Koran, surah XXIV: 45

CREATION ACCORDING TO NORSE MYTHOLOGY

"Odin and his brothers, Vili and Ve, decided to make people for the world. They created the first man from a living ash tree and named him Ask, for the tree from which he was made. Odin gave him his life and soul. Vili gave him the five senses and the power of motion, and Ve made the blood run in his veins. They created the first woman in the same way, from a living elm tree and named her Embla. Odin endowed her with life and soul. Vili gave her motion and senses; Ve gave her her blood."
Maria Leach. *The Beginning: Creation Myths around the World.* New York: Funk & Wagnalls, 1956.

CREATION ACCORDING TO THE MAYA-QUICHÉ OF GUATEMALA

"The gods made the blood of man from water, his arms and legs and body from yellow corn ears and white corn ears. The first four men were fine men, wonderful men. They spoke and walked; they could see so far that they saw the whole world at once and on into the stars. They understood all things. So the gods remade them. The gods dimmed their sight so they could see only nearby. And they took from them also their understanding."
Adapted from the *Popol Vu.* Oklahoma University Press, Norman, 1950.

WHICH RELIGION FOR LUCY?

CREATION ACCORDING TO THE HOPI TRIBE OF ARIZONA
"Spider Woman gathered earth, this time of four colors, yellow, red, white, and black; mixed with *túchvala*, the liquid of her mouth; molded them; and covered them with her white-substance cape, which was the creative wisdom itself . . . she sang over them the Creation Song, and when she uncovered them these forms were human beings in the image of Sótuknang. Then she created four other beings after her own form. They were *wúti*, female partners, for the first four male beings."
Frank Waters. *Book of the Hopi*, New York: The Viking Press, 1963.

CREATION ACCORDING TO THE HAIDA INDIANS OF THE QUEEN CHARLOTTE ISLANDS, BRITISH COLUMBIA
"Not long ago, there was nothing but open sea. And Raven was flying. Then one little small rocky island was in the sea, and Raven sat upon it. 'Become earth,' he said, and it became the earth. Raven was a god in those days. . . . One day he was walking along in the sand at the edge of the water, alone in the empty world, and heard a small sound. He listened . . . A clamshell was sticking up . . . Raven bent down and looked into it. He saw a little human face. 'Come out,' he whispered. . . . Thus Raven drew mankind out of a clamshell and the world was peopled."
Maria Leach, *The Beginning*.

CREATION IN GREEK MYTHOLOGY
"To Prometheus and his brother Epimetheus was now committed the office of making man and providing him and all other animals with the faculties necessary for their preservation. . . . Epimetheus proceeded to bestow upon the different animals the various gifts of courage, strength, swiftness, sagacity; wings to one, claws to another, a shelly covering to a third. But Prometheus himself made a nobler animal than these. Taking some earth and kneading it with water, he made man in the image of the gods. He gave him an upright stature, so that while other animals turn their faces toward the earth, man gazes on the stars. Then since Epimetheus . . . had been so prodigal of his gifts to other animals that no blessing was left worth conferring upon the noblest of creatures, Prometheus ascended to heaven, lit his torch at the chariot of the sun, and brought down fire. With fire in his possession man would be able to win secrets and treasures from the earth, to develop commerce, science, and the arts."
Charles M. Gayley. *The Classic Myths*. Lexington, Mass., Toronto: Xerox College Publications, 1939.

CREATION ACCORDING TO THE MUNDURUCU' INDIANS OF BRAZIL
"Karusakaibö made the world one day, but he did not get as far as making mankind. Karusakaibö was alone in the world except for Daiiru, the armadillo, who was his helper and companion. One day Daiiru offended the creator in some way, and Karusakaibö was so enraged that Daiiru hid in a hole in the ground. . . . Karusakaibö blew into the hole with a great gust of wind and stamped his foot upon the earth with such force that Daiiru was blown out of the hole into the air. When he landed on the earth he said, 'There are people down there!' . . . 'We must get them out,' said Karusakaibö. So Karusakaibö and Daiiru . . . made a cotton rope . . . The people climbed up the rope one by one, but many, many came out. When half of them had climbed out into the world, the rope broke and the rest had to stay underground. They are there yet. The sun shines in their country when it is night in this world."
Maria Leach, *The Beginning*.

CREATION ACCORDING TO THE ABORIGINES OF AUSTRALIA
"In the beginning at first, in the dream time, the Ancestors emerged from the earth somewhere 'to the north' and wandered the dream path, stopping now and then at billabongs (waterholes) now called story places, because here they stopped to create food plants, or certain animals, or to fix up the landscape to their liking."
Maria Leach, *The Beginning*.

CREATION ACCORDING TO THE FANS, A WESTERN BANTU PEOPLE OF EQUATORIAL AFRICA
"Mbere, the creator, made a man out of clay, but first he was a lizard. Mbere put the lizard in the great big sea water. He left him there five days. On the fifth day Mbere looked and the lizard was in there. On the seventh day Mbere looked and the lizard was in there. On the eighth day Mbere looked and the lizard came out. But when he came out he was a man. 'Thank you,' said the man to Mbere."
Maria Leach, *The Beginning*.

CREATION IN INDIA
"At first Kujum-Chantu, the earth, was like a human being; she had a head, and arms and legs, and an enormous fat belly. The original human begins lived on the surface of her belly. One day it occurred to Kujum-Chantu that if she ever got up and walked about, everyone would fall off and be killed, so she herself died of her own accord. Her head became the snow-covered mountains, the bones of her back turned into smaller hills . . ."
Maria Leach, *The Beginning*.
OR
"Verily, in the beginning this universe was water, nothing but a sea of water. The waters desired, 'How can we be reproduced?' They toiled and performed fervid devotions. When they were heated, a golden egg was produced. The year, indeed, was not then in existence; this golden egg floated about for as long as the space of a year. In a year's time a man . . . was produced therefrom."
Charles H. Long. *Alpha: The Myths of Creation*. New York: George Braziller, 1963.

A bit of cosmogony never harmed anybody.

1 My jaws were stronger than those of a chimpanzee.

TRUE ☐ ☐ FALSE

2 I loved to go "fishing" for termites.

TRUE ☐ ☐ FALSE

3 I was about as tall as a nine-year-old girl.

TRUE ☐ ☐ FALSE

4 I had a nice wardrobe.

TRUE ☐ ☐ FALSE

5 I'm the missing link.

TRUE ☐ ☐ FALSE

11 I am a hominid.

TRUE ☐ ☐ FALSE

12 In my day, Ethiopia was a lot greener.

TRUE ☐ ☐ FALSE

13 Louis and I lived in a cave.

TRUE ☐ ☐ FALSE

14 I lived about 300,000 years ago.

TRUE ☐ ☐ FALSE

15 I took long walks on the savanna.

TRUE ☐ ☐ FALSE

ONE POINT FOR EVERY RIGHT ANSWER

	OH, MY!	SAPIENS?	SO-SO	VERY GOOD	EXCELLENT

0 pts   4 pts   8 pts   10 pts   16 pts   20 p

SAPIENS SAPIENS?

To find out, answer these questions

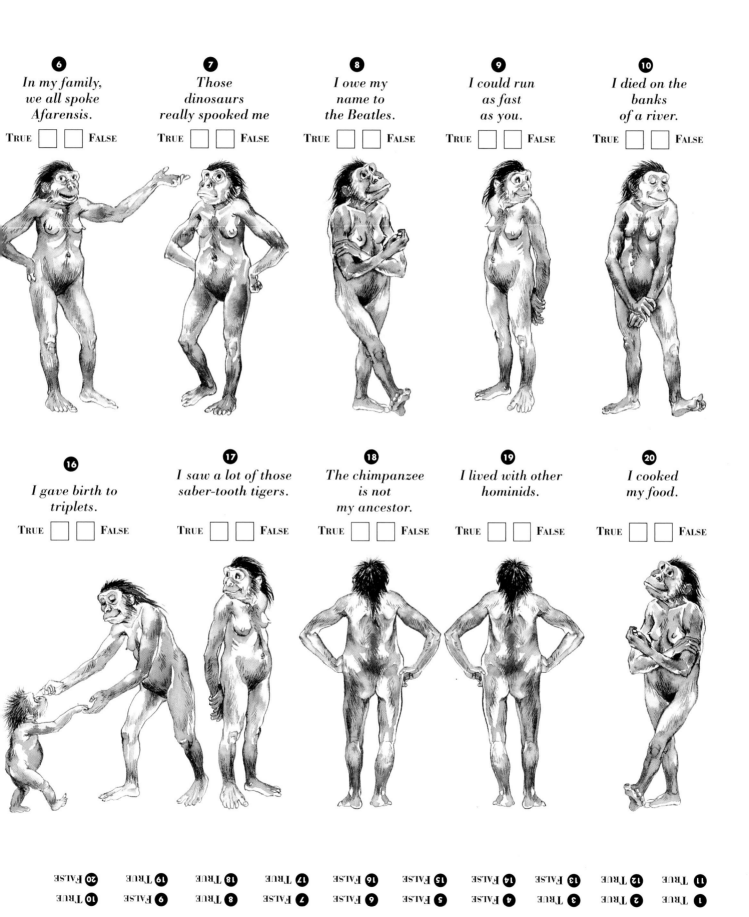

6
In my family,
we all spoke
Afarensis.

TRUE ☐ ☐ FALSE

7
Those
dinosaurs
really spooked me

TRUE ☐ ☐ FALSE

8
I owe my
name to
the Beatles.

TRUE ☐ ☐ FALSE

9
I could run
as fast
as you.

TRUE ☐ ☐ FALSE

10
I died on the
banks
of a river.

TRUE ☐ ☐ FALSE

16
I gave birth to
triplets.

TRUE ☐ ☐ FALSE

17
I saw a lot of those
saber-tooth tigers.

TRUE ☐ ☐ FALSE

18
The chimpanzee
is not
my ancestor.

TRUE ☐ ☐ FALSE

19
I lived with other
hominids.

TRUE ☐ ☐ FALSE

20
I cooked
my food.

TRUE ☐ ☐ FALSE

20 FALSE **19** TRUE **18** TRUE **17** TRUE **16** FALSE **15** FALSE **14** FALSE **13** FALSE **12** TRUE **11** TRUE

10 TRUE **9** FALSE **8** TRUE **7** FALSE **6** FALSE **5** FALSE **4** FALSE **3** TRUE **2** TRUE **1** TRUE

INDEX

BOOKS FOR FURTHER READING

Facchini, Fiorenzo. Translated by Rocco Serini. *Humans: Origins & Evolution*. Chatham, N.J.: Raintree Steck-Vaughn, 1994.

Johanson, Donald. *Ancestors: The Search for Our Human Origins*. New York: Random House, 1994.

Journey from the Dawn: Life with the World's First Family. New York: Random House, 1990.

Lewin, Roger. *In the Age of Mankind: A Smithsonian Book of Human Evolution*. Washington, D.C.: Smithsonian Institute Press, 1989.

Lindsay, William. *Prehistoric Life*. New York: Knopf, 1994.

Lucy—Beginnings of Humankind. New York: Simon & Schuster, 1990.

Lucy's Child: The Discovery of a Human Ancestor. New York: Avon, 1990.

Milner, Richard. *Encyclopedia of Evolution*. New York: Henry Holt, 1993.

The Origin of Modern Humans. New York: W.H. Freeman, 1995.

Tattersall, Ian. *The Human Odyssey: Four Million Years of Human Evolution*. New York: Simon & Schuster, 1993.

The Visual Dictionary of Prehistoric Life. New York: Dorling Kindersley, 1995.

ILLUSTRATIONS

PHOTOGRAPHS

PHOTO CREDITS